COMPREHENSIVE GUIDE TO GENERIC PRODUCT DEVELOPMENT

THEORY AND PRACTICE

VEERAREDDY PRABHAKAR REDDY,
MURALIDHAR RAO AKKALADEVI

Contents

Contents

Preface

The pharmaceutical industry plays a crucial role in ensuring access to affordable and effective medicines for people worldwide. Among the significant contributors to this accessibility are generic drugs, which provide high-quality alternatives to brand-name medicines at reduced costs. **This book, "Comprehensive Guide to Generic Product Development: Theory and Practice," is designed to offer a complete understanding of the scientific, regulatory, and practical aspects of generic drug development.**

The journey of a generic drug, from its concept to its availability in the market, is a complex process requiring expertise in formulation, analytical method development, regulatory compliance, and quality assurance. With the growing emphasis on global harmonization of drug standards and increasing demand for generic medicines, it is essential to have a well-structured guide that addresses these multifaceted areas comprehensively.

This book is written for students, academicians, and industry professionals who are keen to learn or refine their knowledge in generic product development. The chapters are organized systematically, covering topics such as preformulation studies, bioequivalence testing, process development, regulatory pathways, and quality management. Real-world case studies and practical examples are included to bridge the gap between theory and practice, making this book an effective learning tool.

One of the unique aspects of this book is its focus on **global regulatory perspectives,** such as guidelines from the **FDA, EMA, and CDSCO,** and the role of international harmonization under the **ICH framework.** It also explores recent advancements in the field, including Quality by Design (QbD), Biopharmaceutics Classification System (BCS)-based waivers, and innovative technologies like 3D printing and nanotechnology.

We believe this book will serve as a valuable resource for all readers, providing clarity on complex topics and fostering a deeper understanding of the critical steps involved in generic drug development. It reflects our sincere efforts to contribute to the growing body of knowledge in pharmaceutical sciences and support the development of professionals dedicated to this field.

We extend our heartfelt gratitude to the mentors, colleagues, and students who have inspired and supported us during the creation of this book. We hope it serves its purpose of guiding and educating future scientists, researchers, and practitioners.

Authors

Veerareddy Prabhakar Reddy

Muralidhar Rao Akkaladevi

Comprehensive Guide To Generic Product Development-theory And Practice

Dr. Prabhakar Reddy Veerareddy
Head, University College of Pharmaceutical Sciences,
Palamuru University,
Mahabubnagar, Telangana, India
Dr. Muralidhar Rao Akkaladevi
Principal, St. Mary's College of Pharmacy,
Secunderabad, Telangana, India

Published by Notion Press
Notion Press, Inc.
800, West El Camino Real #180,
California, USA 94040
Notion Press Media Pvt Ltd
#7, Red Cross Road,
Egmore, Chennai, Tamil Nadu 600008
Email ID: publish@notionpress.com
Phone Number: +91 44 46315631

CHAPTER ONE

Introduction to Generic Drug Development

1.1 Definition of Generic Drugs

1.1.1 Generic vs. Brand-name Drugs

A **generic drug** is a medication that has the same active ingredients, strength, dosage form, route of administration, and therapeutic effect as a brand-name drug. Generic drugs are considered **bioequivalent** to their brand-name counterparts, meaning they work in the same way and provide the same clinical benefit. However, the key difference lies in the cost and the **regulatory pathway** required for approval. Brand-name drugs undergo extensive research, clinical trials, and patent protection, whereas generic drugs can bypass this expensive process by proving bioequivalence through the **Abbreviated New Drug Application (ANDA)** process.

While **brand-name drugs** are typically developed after years of research and receive patent protection to ensure exclusivity, once the patent expires, generic manufacturers can apply for approval, reducing the overall cost of the drug. Brand-name drugs often command higher prices due to the cost recovery of research, development, and marketing. In contrast, generic drugs are significantly cheaper since they do not bear the same research and development costs.

For example, **Lipitor® (Atorvastatin)**, a popular cholesterol-lowering medication, was sold at a high price until its patent expired. Afterward, multiple generic versions of atorvastatin became available, offering patients a much more affordable option with the same therapeutic effect. Similarly, **metformin**, an essential drug for diabetes management, is widely available in its generic form, ensuring affordability for patients worldwide.

The differences in the regulatory requirements for generics and brand-name drugs are critical in understanding why generics are more affordable.

While brand-name drugs must demonstrate **safety and efficacy** through extensive clinical trials, generic drugs need only prove **bioequivalence** to the brand-name drug. This difference allows generics to be introduced to the market faster and at a lower cost.

1.1.2 Characteristics and Benefits of Generics

Generic drugs must be identical or bioequivalent to their brand-name counterparts in terms of **active ingredient**, dosage form, strength, route of administration, and intended use. However, there can be minor differences in excipients such as fillers, binders, or colorings. These differences do not affect the safety or efficacy of the drug but allow manufacturers to differentiate their product in terms of appearance, while ensuring the same therapeutic effect.

The main benefit of generic drugs is their **affordability**. Because generic manufacturers do not need to invest in costly research and development, they can sell their products at a fraction of the price of brand-name drugs. On average, generic drugs cost **80% to 85% less** than brand-name medications, making them more accessible to a wider population, particularly in low- and middle-income countries.

According to a report from the **Association for Accessible Medicines (AAM)**, in the United States alone, generic drugs saved the healthcare system **USD 338 billion** in 2022. Similarly, in India, where the government has promoted the use of generic medicines under initiatives like **Pradhan Mantri Bhartiya Janaushadhi Pariyojana (PMBJP)**, generics account for nearly **70%** of the total pharmaceutical market. These cost savings are crucial, particularly for the treatment of **chronic diseases** like hypertension, diabetes, and cancer, where long-term medication adherence is essential for managing the condition.

The introduction of generics also encourages **market competition**, which further drives down drug prices. For example, after the patent for **sildenafil (Viagra®)** expired, the introduction of generic versions led to a **50% price reduction** within a few months. This price drop significantly increased patient access to this essential medication for erectile dysfunction.

Generics not only benefit patients but also reduce the overall financial burden on **healthcare systems**. Public health programs like **Medicare** and **Medicaid** in the U.S., and similar schemes in India and other countries, rely heavily on generic drugs to manage costs while providing high-quality care to patients.

1.2 Global Overview of Generic Drugs

1.2.1 Importance of Generic Drugs in Global Healthcare

Generic drugs play a critical role in ensuring **universal access** to affordable medicines across the world. In developing countries, where the healthcare infrastructure is limited, generics often provide the only feasible option for patients who cannot afford brand-name medications. Generics have been instrumental in addressing the global burden of **communicable diseases** like **HIV/AIDS** and **tuberculosis**, where access to affordable treatment is essential for disease control.

For instance, the global fight against HIV/AIDS has seen immense success with the availability of generic versions of **antiretroviral drugs (ARVs)**. India, known as the "pharmacy of the world," produces more than **80%** of the world's generic ARVs, making these life-saving treatments available to millions of people in low-income countries. Generic drugs have also played a key role in the **World Health Organization's (WHO)** initiative to eliminate neglected tropical diseases (NTDs) by providing affordable treatment options for diseases like **schistosomiasis** and **leprosy**.

In the developed world, generic drugs have become an indispensable part of healthcare systems. In the U.S., generic drugs account for more than **85%** of all prescriptions, providing substantial savings to both patients and insurers. The **U.S. FDA** has streamlined the process for approving generic drugs through the **Generic Drug User Fee Amendments (GDUFA)**, enabling faster access to generics and driving competition.

In India, where **out-of-pocket expenditure** accounts for a large share of healthcare spending, the government's push toward **Jan Aushadhi Kendras** has provided patients with access to high-quality generics at significantly lower prices. These initiatives have made essential medicines for chronic conditions like **hypertension, diabetes**, and **asthma** more affordable for millions of patients.

The **global generic pharmaceutical market** was valued at approximately **USD 370 billion** in 2023 and is expected to grow at a compound annual growth rate (CAGR) of **6.1%** between 2024 and 2030. This growth is driven by factors such as patent expirations of major brand-name drugs, an increasing burden of chronic diseases, and rising healthcare costs, which compel governments and health systems to seek cost-effective treatment options.

1.2.2 Market Trends and Future Outlook

The generic drug market is experiencing significant growth due to an increasing number of **patent expirations**, which has opened opportunities for generic manufacturers to introduce cost-effective alternatives to some of the world's most commonly prescribed medications. A key trend in the industry is the growing demand for **biosimilars**, which are generic versions of **biologic drugs**. Biologics, which are derived from living cells, represent some of the most advanced treatments available today, but they are often prohibitively expensive. Biosimilars provide a more affordable alternative, offering similar therapeutic effects at a fraction of the cost.

According to **IQVIA**, biosimilars are expected to save the global healthcare system **USD 100 billion** by 2025. In regions like Europe, where the **European Medicines Agency (EMA)** has been leading the approval of biosimilars, these drugs have already made significant inroads into the market. The introduction of biosimilars for conditions like **rheumatoid arthritis**, **diabetes**, and **cancer** is expected to further drive the growth of the generic drug market.

In the **Indian generic drug market**, companies like **Sun Pharma, Cipla,** and **Dr. Reddy's Laboratories** are at the forefront of the global generic supply chain. India's generic pharmaceutical exports were valued at **USD 24.5 billion** in 2023, with exports to key markets such as the U.S., Africa, and Southeast Asia.

As the demand for generics grows, so do the challenges. Generic manufacturers must navigate complex **regulatory requirements** across different regions. While the U.S. and Europe have well-established pathways for the approval of generic drugs, emerging markets still face regulatory bottlenecks. Additionally, the issue of **patent evergreening**—a strategy used by brand-name manufacturers to extend the life of their patents by making minor modifications to the original drug—poses a challenge to the timely introduction of generics.

The future of the generic drug industry will be shaped by the rise of **digital health technologies, 3D printing,** and **nanotechnology,** which promise to revolutionize drug development and manufacturing. **3D printing** of drugs, for instance, allows for the precise manufacturing of personalized medications, while **nanotechnology** enables the development of more effective drug delivery systems, particularly for poorly soluble drugs. These innovations will likely expand the scope of generic drugs, allowing for more sophisticated and tailored treatments at lower costs.

1.3 History and Evolution of Generic Drug Development

1.3.1 Milestones in the U.S.

The evolution of the generic drug industry in the United States has been shaped by a series of important legislative milestones. The **1938 Federal Food, Drug, and Cosmetic Act (FDCA)** marked the first significant shift in drug regulation, requiring pharmaceutical companies to prove the safety of their products before marketing them. However, it wasn't until the passage of the **1962 Kefauver-Harris Amendments** that efficacy became a mandatory requirement. These amendments followed the **thalidomide tragedy**, which highlighted the importance of ensuring both safety and efficacy in pharmaceutical products.

The most pivotal moment in the history of generic drugs came with the passage of the **Hatch-Waxman Act** in 1984. The **Hatch-Waxman Act**, also known as the **Drug Price Competition and Patent Term Restoration Act**, established the **Abbreviated New Drug Application (ANDA)** pathway, which allowed generic manufacturers to prove **bioequivalence** to brand-name drugs without conducting expensive clinical trials. This legislation also introduced the concept of **patent term extensions** to compensate brand-name manufacturers for the time lost during the FDA approval process, striking a balance between incentivizing innovation and promoting generic competition.

Since the passage of the Hatch-Waxman Act, the U.S. generic drug market has expanded rapidly. In 1984, generics accounted for just **19%** of all prescriptions. By 2023, this number had grown to over **85%**, thanks in large part to the streamlined approval process and the efforts of the **FDA's Office of Generic Drugs (OGD)**.

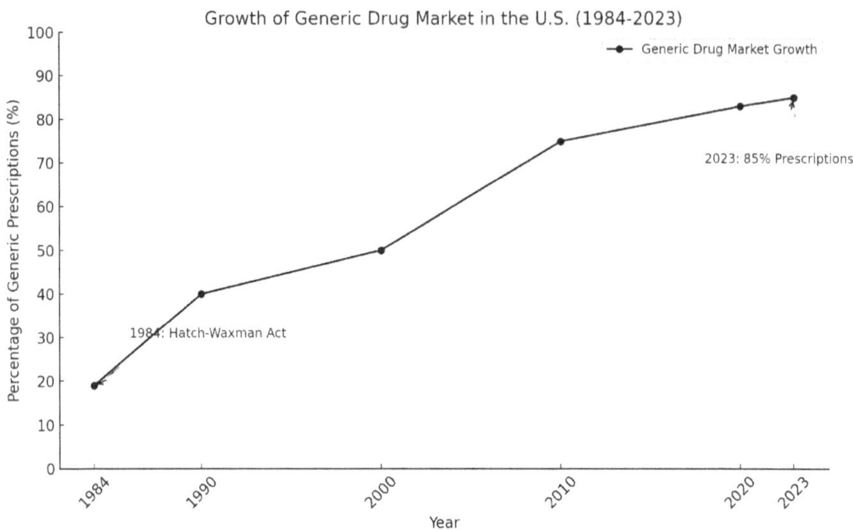

Growth of the generic drug market in the U.S. from 1984 to 2023: 1984: 19% generic prescriptions (Hatch-Waxman Act introduced the ANDA pathway). 2023: 85% generic prescriptions.

1.3.2 Milestones Worldwide

Outside the United States, the growth of the generic drug industry has been equally transformative. In Europe, the establishment of the **European Medicines Agency (EMA)** in 1995 created a centralized system for drug approvals, which has significantly accelerated the introduction of generic drugs across the European Union. By harmonizing regulations and ensuring a high standard for safety and efficacy, the EMA has facilitated the widespread adoption of generics.

India has emerged as the world's largest supplier of generic medicines, accounting for **20%** of the global generic drug supply by volume. The **1984 Drugs Price Control Order** and subsequent policies have promoted the production of affordable medicines in India, turning the country into a global leader in generic pharmaceuticals. The growth of companies like **Sun Pharma**, **Cipla**, and **Lupin** has cemented India's reputation as the "pharmacy of the world."

Global trade agreements such as the **Trade-Related Aspects of Intellectual Property Rights (TRIPS)** agreement have played a significant role in shaping the development of generics. While TRIPS introduced stronger intellectual property protections, it also included provisions for **compulsory licensing**, which allows governments to authorize the production of generic versions of patented drugs in public health emergencies. This provision has been crucial in ensuring access to affordable medicines in low-income countries, particularly for diseases like HIV/AIDS, malaria, and tuberculosis.

The availability of generics has had a profound impact on the treatment of **HIV/AIDS**. In the early 2000s, the annual cost of antiretroviral therapy (ART) was over **USD 10,000** per patient in developed countries. However, thanks to the production of generic ARVs, the cost of treatment has dropped to less than **USD 100** per patient per year in many developing countries, saving millions of lives.

CHAPTER TWO

The Hatch-Waxman Act and Its Impact

2.1 Overview of the Hatch-Waxman Act (1984)

2.1.1 Key Provisions of the Hatch-Waxman Act

The **Hatch-Waxman Act of 1984**, formally known as the **Drug Price Competition and Patent Term Restoration Act**, was a landmark piece of legislation that reshaped the pharmaceutical industry in the United States. The Act aimed to balance two seemingly conflicting goals: 1) promoting **innovation** by protecting the intellectual property rights of **brand-name drug manufacturers**, and 2) enhancing **access** to affordable medicines by simplifying the approval process for **generic drug manufacturers**.

One of the key provisions of the Hatch-Waxman Act was the establishment of the **Abbreviated New Drug Application (ANDA)** process. This allowed generic manufacturers to bypass the costly and time-consuming process of conducting new clinical trials for safety and efficacy, which brand-name drugs are required to undergo. Instead, generic manufacturers need only prove **bioequivalence** to the brand-name drug, which means that the generic drug works in the same way and delivers the same therapeutic effect as its branded counterpart.

The Act also introduced **patent term extensions** to compensate brand-name drug companies for time lost during the FDA approval process. This extension could add up to five years of exclusivity to a drug's patent, but the total patent life of the drug could not exceed **14 years** from the date of approval.

Moreover, the Hatch-Waxman Act created the concept of **market exclusivity** for generic manufacturers. The first generic company to successfully challenge a brand-name drug's patent was granted **180 days of market exclusivity**, during which no other generic versions could enter the market. This provision provided a significant financial incentive for generic manufacturers to challenge weak or invalid patents.

Overall, the Hatch-Waxman Act is credited with creating the modern **generic drug industry**. It fostered competition, leading to lower drug prices and improved access to essential medications. By 2023, generic drugs accounted for over **85%** of all prescriptions in the U.S., saving the healthcare system billions of dollars annually.

2.1.2 Importance of the Hatch-Waxman Act in Generic Development

The importance of the Hatch-Waxman Act in the development of the generic drug industry cannot be overstated. Before 1984, the process of developing a generic version of a drug was prohibitively expensive and slow. Generic manufacturers were required to repeat much of the clinical research that brand-name companies had already conducted, making the process both inefficient and costly.

The introduction of the ANDA process changed this dynamic by allowing generics to enter the market much faster and at a fraction of the cost. By proving bioequivalence instead of conducting full clinical trials, generic manufacturers could bring drugs to market more efficiently, which significantly reduced the **time to market** and lowered costs for consumers.

According to the **Generic Pharmaceutical Association (GPhA)**, generic drugs saved the U.S. healthcare system an estimated **USD 338 billion** in 2022 alone. The availability of generic drugs has also increased patient adherence to treatment, particularly in cases where chronic medications are needed. For example, drugs for managing **hypertension**, **diabetes**, and **cholesterol** are now widely available as generics, significantly reducing the overall cost of care.

The Hatch-Waxman Act also introduced a mechanism for resolving patent disputes, known as **Paragraph IV certifications**. This allowed generic manufacturers to challenge the patents of brand-name drugs before their expiration. These patent challenges have resulted in many generic versions reaching the market earlier than expected, contributing to further reductions in healthcare costs.

Since the passage of the Hatch-Waxman Act, the number of ANDAs filed annually has increased dramatically. In **1984**, fewer than **20%** of all prescriptions were filled with generic drugs. By **2023**, that number had risen to over **85%**, reflecting the Act's profound impact on drug affordability and accessibility.

2.2 Amendments to the Hatch-Waxman Act

2.2.1 Key Amendments to the Hatch-Waxman Act

Since its passage in 1984, the Hatch-Waxman Act has been amended several times to address challenges in balancing patent protection with the need for affordable generic medicines. One of the most significant amendments was the **Medicare Prescription Drug, Improvement, and Modernization Act (MMA) of 2003**. This law aimed to curb the abuse of the **30-month stay** provision, which allowed brand-name manufacturers to delay the approval of generic drugs by challenging the patent through legal means. The MMA limited the number of automatic 30-month stays to **one per generic drug application**, ensuring that generic entry could not be indefinitely delayed through multiple patent challenges.

Another important amendment came with the passage of the **FDA Amendments Act of 2007**, which strengthened the FDA's authority to ensure the **safety** of both brand-name and generic drugs. The Act introduced **Risk Evaluation and Mitigation Strategies (REMS)**, which were designed to monitor the safety of drugs once they were on the market. This amendment had a significant impact on generic manufacturers, as it required them to comply with the same REMS programs as the brand-name manufacturers.

In **2012**, the introduction of the **Generic Drug User Fee Amendments (GDUFA)** further streamlined the generic drug approval process by allowing the FDA to collect fees from generic manufacturers to fund the review of ANDAs. The additional resources provided by GDUFA helped the FDA reduce the backlog of generic drug applications and shorten review times.

These amendments have ensured that the Hatch-Waxman framework remains relevant in a rapidly evolving pharmaceutical landscape, where innovation and access must be carefully balanced.

2.2.2 Impact on Patent Litigation

The Hatch-Waxman Act fundamentally changed the way **patent litigation** is handled in the pharmaceutical industry. Before 1984, generic manufacturers had little incentive to challenge the patents of brand-name drugs. The Hatch-Waxman Act introduced the concept of **Paragraph IV certifications**, which allow a generic manufacturer to challenge a brand-name drug's patent by asserting that the patent is either invalid or unenforceable, or that the generic product does not infringe the patent.

When a generic manufacturer files a Paragraph IV certification, it must notify the brand-name manufacturer, who then has **45 days** to file a **patent**

infringement lawsuit. If the lawsuit is filed, the FDA automatically grants a **30-month stay** of the generic drug's approval, giving the brand-name company time to defend its patent in court.

The **Paragraph IV certification** process has led to a significant increase in patent litigation between brand-name and generic manufacturers. According to the **FDA**, as of **2020**, more than **80%** of all patent litigation in the pharmaceutical industry involved Paragraph IV certifications. The result of these lawsuits can determine whether a generic drug enters the market early or must wait until the brand-name drug's patent expires.

Pay-for-delay agreements, where brand-name manufacturers pay generic companies to delay the introduction of a generic version, have become a controversial aspect of Hatch-Waxman litigation. These settlements can prevent generics from entering the market for years, costing consumers billions of dollars in higher drug prices. The **Federal Trade Commission (FTC)** has estimated that pay-for-delay agreements cost U.S. consumers **USD 3.5 billion** annually in higher drug costs.

2.2.3 Market Exclusivity

The Hatch-Waxman Act also introduced the concept of **market exclusivity** for generic manufacturers. The first generic manufacturer to file a Paragraph IV certification and successfully challenge the patent of a brand-name drug is granted **180 days of market exclusivity**. During this period, no other generic versions can be approved, allowing the first-filer to capture a large share of the market and recoup the costs of challenging the patent.

This **180-day exclusivity period** has proven to be a significant incentive for generic manufacturers to challenge patents aggressively. For example, in the case of **omeprazole (Prilosec®)**, the first generic manufacturer to successfully challenge the patent earned **USD 175 million** in revenue during the exclusivity period, before competition from other generics entered the market.

However, the exclusivity period is not without its challenges. In some cases, first-filers have entered into **settlement agreements** with brand-name manufacturers to delay the launch of their generic drugs. These agreements, known as **pay-for-delay** settlements, have sparked legal and regulatory debates, as they can prevent other generics from entering the market and keep drug prices high.

The **FTC** has challenged several of these agreements, arguing that they violate **antitrust laws** by restricting competition. In the **FTC v. Actavis,**

Inc. decision in 2013, the U.S. Supreme Court ruled that pay-for-delay agreements could be subject to antitrust scrutiny, setting an important precedent for future litigation.

2.3 Regulatory and Legal Framework Post Hatch-Waxman

2.3.1 Abbreviated New Drug Application (ANDA)

The **Abbreviated New Drug Application (ANDA)** process, introduced by the Hatch-Waxman Act, has significantly streamlined the approval of generic drugs. Unlike brand-name drugs, which must undergo extensive clinical trials to prove **safety and efficacy**, generics need only demonstrate **bioequivalence** to the Reference Listed Drug (RLD). This means that the generic drug delivers the same **active ingredient** to the body at the same rate and to the same extent as the brand-name drug.

The ANDA submission requires data on the drug's **formulation, manufacturing process**, and **bioequivalence studies**. The generic manufacturer must also demonstrate that its product meets the same **quality standards** as the brand-name drug, including purity, potency, and stability.

Since the introduction of the ANDA process, the FDA has approved thousands of generic drugs, leading to significant savings for consumers. According to the **FDA's Office of Generic Drugs**, the agency approved **735 ANDAs** in 2022 alone, a significant increase from the **19 ANDAs** approved in 1984, the year the Hatch-Waxman Act was passed.

The introduction of the **Generic Drug User Fee Amendments (GDUFA)** in 2012 has further accelerated the ANDA approval process by providing the FDA with additional resources to review applications. Under GDUFA, generic manufacturers pay fees to help fund the review process, allowing the FDA to reduce review times and clear the backlog of ANDA submissions.

2.3.2 Paragraph IV Certifications

The **Paragraph IV certification** process, introduced by the Hatch-Waxman Act, has played a central role in the generic drug industry's ability to challenge the patents of brand-name drugs. When filing an ANDA, a generic manufacturer can submit a Paragraph IV certification, asserting that the brand-name drug's patent is invalid, unenforceable, or not infringed by the generic product.

If the brand-name manufacturer disagrees, it has **45 days** to file a **patent infringement lawsuit**. This lawsuit triggers an automatic **30-month stay** of the generic drug's approval, giving the brand-name company time to defend its patent in court. If the court rules in favor of the generic manufacturer, the FDA can approve the generic drug even before the patent expires.

Paragraph IV certifications have become a crucial tool for generic manufacturers looking to bring their products to market earlier than the brand-name drug's patent expiration. Some of the most notable **Paragraph IV challenges** include the case of **Clopidogrel (Plavix®)**, where generic manufacturers successfully invalidated key patents, allowing generics to enter the market years ahead of schedule.

The **FTC** closely monitors Paragraph IV litigation, particularly in cases where **pay-for-delay settlements** are involved. These settlements, where the brand-name manufacturer pays the generic company to delay the launch of the generic product, have raised antitrust concerns. The **FTC v. Actavis, Inc.** case in 2013 set a precedent for the legality of these settlements, ruling that they could be subject to antitrust scrutiny.

CHAPTER THREE

Regulatory Pathways for Generic Drug Approvals

3.1 The Abbreviated New Drug Application (ANDA) Process
Requirements for Filing an ANDA

The **Abbreviated New Drug Application (ANDA)** is the pathway through which manufacturers seek approval for generic drugs. Unlike the New Drug Application (NDA) process, ANDAs do not require preclinical and clinical data to establish safety and efficacy. Instead, they rely on demonstrating that the generic drug is bioequivalent to an already approved Reference Listed Drug (RLD). Filing an ANDA requires adherence to strict regulatory guidelines to ensure the generic product meets the necessary quality, safety, and therapeutic standards.

Key Requirements for Filing an ANDA:

1. **Demonstration of Bioequivalence:**

   - The generic drug must have the same **active ingredient, dosage form, strength, route of administration**, and **conditions of use** as the RLD.
   - Bioequivalence studies must show that the rate and extent of drug absorption are within an acceptable range, typically **80-125%** of the RLD.
   - Studies include:

     - **Pharmacokinetic (PK) studies:** Measure drug levels in the bloodstream.
     - **Pharmacodynamic (PD) studies:** If PK is insufficient, these studies assess biological effects.

- **In vitro dissolution tests:** Ensure similar release profiles between the generic and the RLD.

2. **Manufacturing Information:**

   - Details of the drug's **formulation**, **composition**, and **manufacturing process** must be provided.
   - The manufacturing site must comply with **Good Manufacturing Practices (GMP)** and undergo inspections by regulatory authorities.

3. **Labeling Requirements:**

   - The generic drug's label must closely match the RLD's label, except for permitted differences, such as the manufacturer's name and contact information.
   - This ensures that healthcare providers and patients receive the same information about the generic product as the RLD.

4. **Patent and Exclusivity Certifications:**

   - ANDA applicants must certify that the generic drug does not infringe existing patents or wait until the patent expires.
   - Certification types include:

     - **Paragraph I:** No patent exists.
     - **Paragraph II:** Patent has expired.
     - **Paragraph III:** Wait for the patent to expire.
     - **Paragraph IV:** Challenges the validity or applicability of a patent.

5. **Drug Master File (DMF):**

   - If using a third-party supplier for active pharmaceutical ingredients (API), a Drug Master File must be submitted detailing API specifications and manufacturing methods.

Review Process and Timelines

The **review process for ANDAs** is designed to ensure that generic drugs meet the stringent requirements for quality, safety, and efficacy without the need for repeating extensive clinical trials. The **Food and Drug Administration (FDA)** oversees this process in the United States, while similar regulatory pathways exist globally, such as the **EMA** in Europe and the **CDSCO** in India.

Steps in the Review Process:

1. **Submission of ANDA:**

   - Applicants submit a complete ANDA, including all necessary data for bioequivalence, manufacturing, labeling, and patents.
   - The FDA checks for **completeness** using the **Filing Review Checklist.**

2. **Initial Review:**

   - The FDA conducts an initial review to ensure all necessary components are present. Missing or insufficient data may result in a **Refuse to Receive (RTR)** letter.

3. **Scientific Review:**

   - The **Office of Generic Drugs (OGD)** reviews the scientific data, including:

     - Bioequivalence studies.
     - Chemistry, Manufacturing, and Controls (CMC) data.
     - Microbiology and stability studies, if applicable.

4. **Facility Inspections:**

   - The FDA inspects manufacturing facilities to confirm compliance with **Current Good Manufacturing Practices (cGMP)**.

5. **Labeling Review:**

   - The proposed labeling is assessed to ensure it aligns with the RLD.

6. **Patent and Exclusivity Review:**

- The FDA examines patent certifications and handles **Paragraph IV challenges**.

Timelines for ANDA Approval:

- Under the **Generic Drug User Fee Amendments (GDUFA)**, the FDA has set specific goals for ANDA review timelines:

  - **Standard ANDA:** 10 months from submission.
  - **Priority ANDA:** 8 months if the drug addresses a public health priority or drug shortage.

- **Real-World Example:**

  - In 2020, the FDA approved over **800 generic drugs**, highlighting the efficiency of the ANDA process.

Challenges During the Review Process:

- **Deficiency Letters:** These are issued when additional information or corrections are needed, potentially delaying approval.
- **Patent Litigation:** Paragraph IV certifications often lead to legal disputes between the generic manufacturer and the RLD holder, which can delay market entry.

Post-Approval Requirements:

- Once approved, generic manufacturers must adhere to strict post-market surveillance, including reporting adverse events and maintaining consistent quality.

Significance of the ANDA Process: The ANDA process plays a vital role in reducing healthcare costs by introducing affordable generic alternatives. By streamlining the approval process and maintaining rigorous standards, regulatory authorities ensure that patients receive high-quality, safe, and effective generic medications.

3.2 Drug Approval Process in the U.S. (FDA)

Key Stages of Generic Drug Approval by the FDA

The **Food and Drug Administration (FDA)** oversees the approval of generic drugs in the United States through a well-defined process that ensures the safety, efficacy, and quality of these medications. The goal is to provide affordable drug alternatives while maintaining the highest standards of public health.

1. Pre-ANDA Meetings:

- Generic drug sponsors can request **Pre-ANDA meetings** with the FDA to discuss specific aspects of their application before submission.
- These meetings provide guidance on:

  - **Bioequivalence study design.**
  - Requirements for Chemistry, Manufacturing, and Controls (**CMC**) data.
  - Addressing potential regulatory or scientific issues.

- **Example:** A manufacturer might seek clarification on the appropriate bioequivalence testing methodology for a highly variable drug.

2. Submission of ANDA:

- The ANDA includes comprehensive data on:

  - **Bioequivalence:** Demonstrating that the generic drug performs similarly to the Reference Listed Drug (**RLD**) in terms of absorption and bioavailability.
  - **CMC:** Details about drug composition, manufacturing processes, and quality controls.
  - **Patent Certifications:** Statements addressing existing patents on the RLD (Paragraph I-IV certifications).
  - **Labeling:** Ensuring the generic drug's label matches the RLD's except for manufacturer-specific details.

- **FDA Filing Review:** The FDA conducts an initial review to ensure the application is complete. If deficiencies are identified, a **Refuse to Receive (RTR)** letter may be issued.

3. Scientific Review:

- **Bioequivalence Review:**

  - Pharmacokinetic studies compare the generic drug's absorption rate and extent to the RLD. Typically, values must fall within the **80-125% range**.
  - In some cases, **pharmacodynamic studies** or in vitro tests are required.

- **CMC Review:**

  - The FDA evaluates the formulation, stability, and manufacturing processes to ensure the drug meets quality standards.

- **Microbiology Review (if applicable):**

  - For sterile products, microbiological tests are critical to confirm safety and sterility.

4. Facility Inspections:

- The FDA inspects the manufacturing facilities to ensure compliance with **Current Good Manufacturing Practices (cGMP)**.
- Inspections cover:

  - Raw material sourcing.
  - Quality control processes.
  - Equipment validation.

5. Labeling Review:

- The FDA ensures that the proposed generic drug labeling aligns with the RLD.
- Minor differences, such as the manufacturer's name, are allowed but must be pre-approved.

6. Patent and Exclusivity Considerations:

- The FDA examines **Paragraph I-IV certifications** to confirm that the generic drug does not infringe on existing patents.
- **Paragraph IV Challenges:**

  - If the ANDA includes a Paragraph IV certification, the RLD holder has **45 days** to file a lawsuit, which may delay FDA approval for **30 months** or until the litigation is resolved.

7. Approval or Tentative Approval:

- If the ANDA meets all scientific, legal, and regulatory requirements, the FDA grants full approval.
- **Tentative Approval:** Issued if the ANDA is ready for approval but cannot be marketed due to unresolved patent or exclusivity issues.

8. Post-Approval Requirements:

- Generic manufacturers must comply with:

  - **Adverse Event Reporting:** Report any post-market safety concerns.
  - **Annual Stability Testing:** Ensure the drug maintains its quality over time.
  - **Regular FDA Inspections:** Confirm ongoing compliance with manufacturing standards.

Timelines for Approval:

- Under the **Generic Drug User Fee Amendments (GDUFA):**

  - **Standard Review:** 10 months from ANDA submission.
  - **Priority Review:** 8 months for drugs addressing shortages or public health needs.

- **Example:** A high-priority generic drug for a cancer treatment might be fast-tracked under the FDA's priority review system.

Significance of the FDA Generic Drug Approval Process:

- Ensures that **generic drugs are as safe and effective** as their branded counterparts.
- Facilitates the introduction of affordable medications, reducing healthcare costs.
- Maintains public trust by adhering to rigorous scientific and regulatory standards.

Real-World Impact:

- In 2021, the FDA approved over **700 generic drugs**, contributing significantly to patient access and affordability. This process underscores the FDA's commitment to balancing innovation with accessibility.

CHAPTER FOUR

Reference Listed Drug (RLD) and Therapeutic Equivalence

4.1 Understanding Reference Listed Drug (RLD)
Definition of Reference Listed Drug (RLD):

- A **Reference Listed Drug (RLD)** is an FDA-approved branded drug product used as the benchmark for developing generic drugs.
- It serves as the **standard for bioequivalence** testing, ensuring that a generic drug is as safe and effective as the original.
- The **Orange Book**, officially titled "Approved Drug Products with Therapeutic Equivalence Evaluations," lists all RLDs, providing manufacturers with information to guide generic drug development.

Key Features of an RLD:

- **Established Safety and Efficacy:**

  - RLDs have undergone extensive clinical trials and regulatory reviews to establish their safety, efficacy, and quality.

- **Benchmark for Generics:**

  - Generic drugs must demonstrate bioequivalence to the RLD, proving they deliver the same therapeutic effect.

- **FDA Listing:**

- The RLD is explicitly identified in the Orange Book for reference in Abbreviated New Drug Applications (ANDAs).

Importance of RLD in Generic Drug Development:

1. **Standard for Bioequivalence Testing:**

   - Generic manufacturers must show that their product is **pharmaceutically equivalent** to the RLD.
   - Bioequivalence studies ensure that the generic's pharmacokinetic (PK) parameters, such as **Cmax** (maximum plasma concentration) and **AUC** (area under the curve), fall within the acceptable range of **80-125%** compared to the RLD.

2. **Guidance for Drug Formulation:**

   - The RLD provides a blueprint for:

     - **Active ingredients.**
     - **Dosage forms** (e.g., tablet, capsule, liquid).
     - **Strengths** and **routes of administration.**

   - This ensures that generics mirror the characteristics of the RLD.

3. **Consistency in Patient Outcomes:**

   - By referencing the RLD, generic drugs are expected to provide the **same therapeutic benefits** and **side effect profiles** as the branded product.
   - This builds confidence among healthcare providers and patients.

4. **Legal and Regulatory Compliance:**

   - RLD designation is crucial for navigating **patent certifications** and ensuring compliance with regulatory standards.
   - ANDA applicants must reference the RLD in their submission to the FDA.

5. **Facilitates Market Entry:**

  ○ The RLD simplifies the approval process for generics, reducing the need for extensive clinical trials.
  ○ This results in faster market entry, making affordable medications available to patients sooner.

Real-World Example:

- **Lipitor (Atorvastatin):**

  ○ Lipitor, a blockbuster statin for cholesterol management, is the RLD for numerous generic versions. Generic manufacturers reference Lipitor to develop bioequivalent statins, ensuring therapeutic consistency at a lower cost.

Significance of RLD in Healthcare:

- **Improves Accessibility:**

  ○ By serving as a benchmark, the RLD enables the development of affordable alternatives, reducing healthcare costs.

- **Ensures Quality and Trust:**

  ○ Standardization ensures that patients receive high-quality, therapeutically equivalent drugs.

- **Encourages Competition:**

  ○ RLD-based generics foster competition in the pharmaceutical market, driving innovation and affordability.

The **Reference Listed Drug (RLD)** is the cornerstone of generic drug development, ensuring that generics meet the same high standards as their branded counterparts. Its role in maintaining safety, efficacy, and therapeutic equivalence is vital for advancing public health.

4.2 Therapeutic Equivalence: Criteria and Evaluation

Therapeutic equivalence refers to the condition where a generic drug not only matches its Reference Listed Drug (RLD) in terms of active ingredients, dosage form, strength, and route of administration but also delivers the same clinical effect and safety profile when used under prescribed conditions. The **FDA** employs rigorous criteria to evaluate therapeutic equivalence, ensuring that generic drugs meet the same high standards of safety, efficacy, and quality as their branded counterparts. This equivalence is critical to guarantee that healthcare providers and patients can trust generics as viable alternatives to branded medications.

The FDA defines therapeutic equivalence using two primary components: **pharmaceutical equivalence** and **bioequivalence**. Pharmaceutical equivalence ensures that the generic drug and its RLD have the same active ingredients, strength, dosage form, and route of administration. However, excipients (inactive ingredients) may differ, provided they do not affect the drug's performance or absorption. Bioequivalence, on the other hand, confirms that the generic drug exhibits comparable pharmacokinetics (PK) to the RLD, such that the rate and extent of absorption are within acceptable limits. The FDA requires that bioequivalence studies demonstrate a **90% confidence interval** for the ratio of the generic drug's **Cmax** (maximum plasma concentration) and **AUC** (area under the plasma concentration-time curve) relative to the RLD to fall within the **80-125% range**. These PK parameters are measured through highly controlled clinical studies conducted on healthy volunteers under fasting or fed conditions, depending on the drug's labeling.

The evaluation process for therapeutic equivalence begins with the submission of an Abbreviated New Drug Application (ANDA), where the generic manufacturer provides comprehensive data demonstrating bioequivalence, manufacturing details, and quality control measures. Bioequivalence studies are pivotal, involving both **in vitro** and **in vivo** assessments. **In vitro dissolution testing** ensures that the drug dissolves at a rate similar to the RLD, while **in vivo studies** measure how the drug is absorbed into the bloodstream. For drugs with narrow therapeutic indices (NTIs), where small differences in drug concentration can lead to therapeutic failure or toxicity, the FDA applies stricter criteria for bioequivalence, often requiring a tighter confidence interval, such as **90-111%** for PK parameters.

Therapeutic equivalence is further evaluated based on the drug's performance characteristics, including its **stability, purity,** and **uniformity.**

The manufacturing facilities of the generic drug must comply with **Current Good Manufacturing Practices (cGMP)**, and the FDA conducts thorough inspections to verify adherence to these standards. In addition, labeling for the generic product must match that of the RLD, except for manufacturer-specific details, ensuring consistency in patient information.

The FDA assigns a **Therapeutic Equivalence (TE) code** in the **Orange Book** to approved generic drugs. Drugs rated as **"AB"** are considered therapeutically equivalent, indicating that bioequivalence has been successfully demonstrated. However, drugs with unresolved bioequivalence issues may receive a "B" rating, indicating that additional data or modifications are needed.

In practice, therapeutic equivalence ensures that generic drugs deliver the same clinical outcomes as their branded counterparts at a significantly lower cost. For instance, **atorvastatin**, a widely prescribed generic for cholesterol management, matches the therapeutic profile of its RLD, **Lipitor**, allowing millions of patients to access affordable treatment without compromising efficacy. The stringent evaluation process conducted by the FDA not only ensures therapeutic consistency but also fosters public confidence in generics. This commitment to rigorous standards makes therapeutic equivalence a cornerstone of healthcare accessibility and affordability, promoting competition and innovation in the pharmaceutical industry.

4.3 Designing Generic Products to Match RLDs

Methods to Ensure Pharmaceutical Equivalence

Designing a generic product to match a Reference Listed Drug (RLD) is a meticulous process that requires adherence to strict regulatory and scientific principles to ensure pharmaceutical equivalence. Pharmaceutical equivalence means that the generic product must have the same **active ingredient(s)**, **dosage form**, **strength**, and **route of administration** as the RLD. While differences in inactive ingredients (excipients) are permissible, they must not affect the drug's safety, efficacy, or bioavailability. Below is a detailed explanation of the methods employed to achieve pharmaceutical equivalence.

1. Selection of the Active Pharmaceutical Ingredient (API):

The first step is ensuring that the generic drug uses the same **API** as the RLD. The API must meet stringent specifications for purity, potency, and stability, as defined in pharmacopoeial standards such as the **USP (United States Pharmacopeia)**. The **polymorphic form** of the API, particle size, and solubility must be consistent with the RLD to ensure equivalent dissolution and absorption rates. For example, in drugs like **glibenclamide**, variations in particle size can significantly impact bioavailability.

2. Formulation Development:

- **Matching the Dosage Form:**

  - The generic drug must replicate the RLD's dosage form (e.g., tablet, capsule, solution). This ensures that the drug is delivered to the body in the same manner.
  - For complex formulations like controlled-release tablets, replicating the drug-release profile is critical.

- **Excipients Selection:**

  - While inactive ingredients can differ, their functionality must remain the same. For instance, **disintegrants**, **binders**, and **stabilizers** used in tablets must replicate the RLD's performance.
  - Careful consideration is given to excipient compatibility to avoid adverse interactions with the API.

- **pH and Osmolarity Adjustment:**

  - For liquid formulations, matching the pH and osmolarity of the RLD is essential to ensure stability and minimize irritation at the site of administration.

3. Analytical Testing for Physical and Chemical Properties:

- **Dissolution Testing:**

  - The dissolution profile of the generic product must closely match that of the RLD. **In vitro dissolution studies** simulate the drug's release in the gastrointestinal tract.
  - Regulatory guidelines typically require that **90% of the generic product dissolves within the same time frame as the RLD under similar conditions.**

- **Stability Testing:**

  - Stability studies are conducted to ensure the generic product maintains its potency and integrity over its shelf life. These tests include accelerated stability studies under varying temperature and humidity conditions.

- **Uniformity of Dosage Units:**

  - Ensuring consistent drug content in each unit (e.g., tablet or capsule) is mandatory. The **content uniformity** must meet regulatory criteria, typically **85-115% of the label claim**.

4. Manufacturing Process Optimization:

- The generic manufacturing process must be designed to replicate the RLD's quality and performance characteristics. This includes:

  - **Granulation and Compression Techniques:** For solid oral dosage forms like tablets.
  - **Mixing and Homogenization:** To ensure even distribution of the API and excipients.
  - **Sterilization Methods:** For injectable products, ensuring sterility is critical.

- Compliance with **Current Good Manufacturing Practices (cGMP)** is essential. The FDA conducts regular inspections to verify adherence to these practices.

5. Bioequivalence Studies:

- Bioequivalence studies compare the generic product's pharmacokinetics with the RLD. These studies include:

  - **Pharmacokinetic (PK) Testing:** Measuring parameters like **Cmax** (maximum plasma concentration) and **AUC** (area under the plasma concentration-time curve) to ensure they fall within the **80-125% range** of the RLD.

- **In Vivo and In Vitro Correlations:** For certain formulations, establishing in vitro–in vivo correlations (IVIVC) is necessary to predict how the drug performs in the body.

6. Matching the Packaging and Labeling:

- **Packaging:**

  - The generic drug's packaging must ensure the same protection and stability as the RLD. This includes using the same material types, such as blister packs or HDPE bottles.
  - For sterile products, maintaining sterility during packaging is essential.

- **Labeling:**

  - The label of the generic product must closely match the RLD, including dosage instructions, warnings, and contraindications. Minor differences, like the manufacturer's name, are allowed but must not impact patient understanding.

7. Compliance with Regulatory Guidelines:

The entire development process must adhere to guidelines set by regulatory authorities such as the FDA. This includes:

- Submission of a comprehensive **Abbreviated New Drug Application (ANDA)**.
- Detailed documentation of bioequivalence, stability studies, and manufacturing processes.
- Regular updates to address any changes in RLD labeling or standards.

Example: For a widely used drug like **omeprazole**, a proton pump inhibitor, manufacturers ensure that the generic capsules meet dissolution criteria by closely replicating the enteric coating used in the RLD. This coating prevents degradation of the drug in stomach acid and ensures release in the intestines.

Designing generic products to match RLDs is a highly structured and regulated process. By employing these methods, manufacturers ensure that generics are **pharmaceutically equivalent** to RLDs, providing patients with safe, effective, and affordable alternatives. This rigorous approach maintains public confidence in the quality of generic drugs while fostering competition and innovation in the pharmaceutical industry.

CHAPTER FIVE

Preformulation Studies in Generic Product Development

5.1 Preformulation: Definition and Importance

Preformulation is the initial stage of product development where the physical, chemical, and mechanical properties of a drug substance are studied. These studies provide the foundational understanding required to design a stable, effective, and manufacturable dosage form. In generic drug development, preformulation studies are critical as they ensure the generic product matches the reference listed drug in terms of quality and performance. By analyzing key parameters, preformulation establishes the groundwork for subsequent formulation design, manufacturing processes, and regulatory compliance. The importance of preformulation lies in identifying potential challenges related to the drug's properties and interactions with excipients, ultimately minimizing risks during development and production.

Key Parameters

Solubility

Solubility is a fundamental parameter studied in preformulation as it directly influences a drug's absorption, bioavailability, and overall therapeutic effect. Solubility assessments involve evaluating the drug's behavior in various solvents, including water, buffers, and organic solvents. Poorly soluble drugs often require strategies such as salt formation, particle size reduction, or the use of solubilizing excipients to enhance their dissolution. For example, weakly acidic or basic drugs may require pH adjustment to optimize their solubility. Additionally, solubility studies help determine whether the drug requires specialized delivery systems like nanoparticles or emulsions to achieve the desired therapeutic concentration.

Stability

Stability studies assess how the drug maintains its integrity under different environmental conditions, including temperature, humidity, light, and oxygen exposure. These studies identify potential degradation pathways and guide the selection of appropriate storage and packaging conditions. For instance, drugs prone to hydrolysis may require protection through desiccants or moisture-proof packaging. Stability studies also involve forced degradation experiments to evaluate how the drug withstands stress conditions, providing insights into its shelf life and the need for stabilizing agents. Long-term stability data are essential for ensuring that the generic product meets quality standards throughout its intended shelf life.

Excipient Compatibility

Excipient compatibility studies evaluate how the drug interacts with inactive ingredients used in the formulation. These studies are crucial because incompatible excipients can cause degradation, alter bioavailability, or affect the physical properties of the final product. For example, certain excipients may accelerate the oxidation of the drug or form insoluble complexes, reducing its efficacy. Compatibility testing involves blending the drug with potential excipients and subjecting the mixtures to stress conditions, such as elevated temperatures or humidity, to observe any changes. The results guide the selection of excipients that ensure stability, manufacturability, and therapeutic consistency.

Preformulation studies are a cornerstone of generic drug development, enabling manufacturers to create products that match the quality, safety, and efficacy of the reference listed drug. By addressing key parameters like solubility, stability, and excipient compatibility, these studies reduce the likelihood of formulation challenges, regulatory delays, and manufacturing failures, ultimately supporting the development of effective and reliable generic medications.

5.2 Characterization of the Active Pharmaceutical Ingredient (API)

Characterizing the active pharmaceutical ingredient is a crucial step in preformulation studies, as it ensures a thorough understanding of the drug's physical and chemical properties. This understanding is fundamental to developing a stable, effective, and manufacturable generic product. Key properties of the API, such as particle size, polymorphism, and others, are carefully evaluated to anticipate and address potential challenges during formulation development, manufacturing, and storage. The insights gained from API characterization help in achieving pharmaceutical equivalence with the reference listed drug and in meeting regulatory standards.

Particle Size

Particle size significantly influences the dissolution rate, bioavailability, and stability of the drug. Smaller particles have a larger surface area, which typically enhances the dissolution rate and absorption, crucial for poorly soluble drugs. However, very fine particles may pose challenges during manufacturing, such as poor flowability and increased risk of aggregation. Particle size analysis is conducted using techniques like laser diffraction or dynamic light scattering. The results guide decisions on whether particle size reduction techniques, such as milling or micronization, are needed to optimize the drug's performance.

Polymorphism

Polymorphism refers to the existence of a drug in multiple crystalline forms, each with distinct physical and chemical properties such as solubility, stability, and melting point. Different polymorphic forms can significantly impact a drug's dissolution rate and bioavailability. For example, one polymorph might dissolve more readily, providing better therapeutic effects, while another might exhibit higher stability, making it more suitable for storage. Polymorphic characterization is performed using techniques like X-ray diffraction, differential scanning calorimetry, and infrared spectroscopy. Identifying and selecting the most appropriate polymorphic form is essential to ensure consistency and therapeutic equivalence with the reference listed drug.

Hygroscopicity

Hygroscopicity refers to the API's ability to absorb moisture from the environment. Highly hygroscopic drugs may degrade or lose stability when exposed to humid conditions, necessitating special packaging or desiccants. Hygroscopicity testing involves exposing the API to various humidity levels and observing its weight gain or physical changes. This characterization helps in determining appropriate storage conditions and the need for moisture-resistant formulations.

Thermal Properties

Thermal properties are assessed to evaluate the API's behavior under different temperature conditions. Thermal analysis techniques like differential scanning calorimetry and thermogravimetric analysis provide insights into melting point, degradation temperature, and heat-related transformations. These data are crucial for designing manufacturing processes that avoid exposing the drug to harmful temperatures and for ensuring the stability of the final product.

Solubility and pH Dependence

Solubility testing determines how readily the API dissolves in various solvents and at different pH levels. The solubility profile is vital for understanding the API's bioavailability and for developing strategies to enhance dissolution for poorly soluble drugs. pH-dependent solubility testing reveals how the drug behaves in different environments, such as the stomach (acidic) and intestines (alkaline), guiding formulation design for optimal release and absorption.

Chemical Stability

Chemical stability tests evaluate the API's susceptibility to degradation under stress conditions such as heat, light, and oxidative environments. These studies identify degradation pathways and guide the selection of stabilizers or protective packaging. For example, light-sensitive drugs may require amber-colored containers to block harmful wavelengths. Stability data are essential for predicting shelf life and ensuring the drug's quality during storage and distribution.

Flow Properties

Flow properties are critical for APIs intended for solid dosage forms like tablets and capsules. Poor flow can result in inconsistent weight and content uniformity during manufacturing. Properties like bulk density, tapped density, and angle of repose are measured to assess flowability. If the flow is inadequate, the addition of flow-enhancing excipients like glidants may be required.

Characterization of the API ensures that its properties align with the requirements for developing a generic product that matches the reference listed drug. By thoroughly analyzing factors such as particle size, polymorphism, hygroscopicity, and others, preformulation studies address potential challenges and establish a strong foundation for successful formulation development and manufacturing. This systematic approach ensures the production of high-quality, stable, and effective generic medications.

5.3 Excipient Compatibility Studies

Excipient compatibility studies are a critical component of preformulation research. These studies evaluate the interactions between the active pharmaceutical ingredient and potential excipients to ensure the stability, efficacy, and manufacturability of the final product. Excipients are inactive ingredients used in formulations to aid in drug delivery, stability, and manufacturing processes. While excipients are considered inert, they can sometimes interact chemically or physically with the active ingredient, leading to degradation, reduced bioavailability, or compromised product performance. Selecting the right excipients through compatibility studies is essential to develop a stable and effective generic product.

Study Objectives

The primary aim of excipient compatibility studies is to identify excipients that do not react negatively with the active ingredient. These studies ensure that the chosen excipients:

- Maintain the stability and potency of the drug over its shelf life.
- Do not alter the drug's dissolution or absorption characteristics.
- Facilitate efficient manufacturing without adverse effects on processability or product performance.

Methodology

Excipient compatibility studies are conducted in a systematic manner to identify any potential interactions under various conditions.

1. **Binary Mixture Screening**:

    - A binary mixture of the active ingredient and each excipient is prepared in predetermined ratios.
    - These mixtures are subjected to stress conditions such as elevated temperatures, humidity, and light exposure.
    - The samples are then analyzed to detect any changes in physical appearance, chemical composition, or stability.

2. **Stress Testing**:

    - Stress tests are designed to accelerate potential interactions. Conditions like 40°C with 75% relative humidity are commonly used.
    - Samples are stored for specific time intervals, such as one week or one month, and evaluated periodically.

3. **Analytical Techniques**:

- Various analytical methods are employed to detect interactions:

  - High-performance liquid chromatography (HPLC) to identify degradation products.
  - Differential scanning calorimetry (DSC) to detect thermal interactions or incompatibilities.
  - Fourier-transform infrared spectroscopy (FTIR) to identify chemical bonding changes.
  - X-ray diffraction (XRD) to assess crystalline structure alterations.

4. **Compatibility Ranking**:

  - Excipients are ranked based on their compatibility with the drug. Those showing no interaction or minimal interaction under stress conditions are selected for formulation development.

Factors Considered in Excipients Selection

1. **Stability**:

  - Excipients should not promote degradation of the active ingredient. For example, lactose, a commonly used filler, may react with drugs containing primary amines, causing the Maillard reaction and resulting in discoloration or loss of potency.

2. **Dissolution and Release**:

  - Excipients must ensure consistent drug release profiles. Poorly soluble drugs may require solubilizers or wetting agents, while controlled-release formulations may use polymers to regulate the release rate.

3. **pH Compatibility**:

  - Certain drugs are stable only within a specific pH range. Excipients like buffers may be required to maintain the desired pH environment for stability.

4. Physical Characteristics:

- Excipients should not alter the physical properties of the formulation, such as compressibility for tablets or viscosity for liquids.

5. Processability:

- Excipients must facilitate efficient manufacturing. For example, lubricants like magnesium stearate improve flowability and prevent sticking during tablet compression.

Case Example

Consider a generic product development for ibuprofen, a widely used anti-inflammatory drug. During compatibility studies, common excipients like microcrystalline cellulose and magnesium stearate were tested. Microcrystalline cellulose showed no significant interaction, while magnesium stearate was found to slow the dissolution rate slightly due to its hydrophobic nature. Adjustments in excipient proportions ensured stability and consistent drug release.

Outcomes

The results of excipient compatibility studies guide the selection of excipients that:

- Enhance the drug's stability and bioavailability.
- Ensure consistent performance under varying environmental conditions.
- Support efficient and reproducible manufacturing processes.

Excipient compatibility studies are an indispensable part of generic product development. By systematically evaluating interactions between the active ingredient and excipients, these studies ensure that the final formulation is stable, effective, and manufacturable. This meticulous approach not only minimizes risks during production and storage but also ensures that the generic product meets stringent regulatory and therapeutic standards.

Formulation Development for Generic Products

6.1 Formulation Design Principles

Formulation design for generic products involves applying scientific and regulatory principles to develop a product that matches the reference listed drug in terms of safety, efficacy, and quality. A key goal of formulation design is to ensure bioequivalence, meaning the generic product delivers the same therapeutic effect as the branded counterpart under identical usage conditions. The principles of formulation design integrate a thorough understanding of the drug's physicochemical properties, excipient functionality, and manufacturing processes to create a stable, effective, and reproducible product.

Core Principles of Formulation Design

1. **Matching the Dosage Form**

   The dosage form of the generic product must be identical to that of the reference listed drug, whether it is a tablet, capsule, suspension, or injection. This ensures that the drug is delivered to the body in the same manner, maintaining consistency in therapeutic outcomes. For example, a controlled-release tablet must replicate the RLD's drug-release profile to achieve equivalent pharmacokinetics.

2. **Bioavailability and Bioequivalence**

   The formulation must ensure that the rate and extent of drug absorption are similar to the RLD. This requires precise control over factors such as particle size, solubility, and dissolution rate. Bioequivalence studies typically assess pharmacokinetic parameters like the maximum plasma concentration (Cmax) and the area under the plasma con7.1centration-time curve (AUC), which must fall within the regulatory range of

80-125%.

3. **Excipient Selection and Functionality**
Excipients play a crucial role in stabilizing the drug, enhancing bioavailability, and ensuring manufacturability. While excipients may differ from those in the RLD, their functionality must remain the same. For instance, disintegrants should ensure similar tablet disintegration times, and binders should provide comparable tablet hardness and integrity.

4. **Solubility and Dissolution**
The dissolution profile of the generic product must closely match that of the RLD. Poorly soluble drugs may require specific techniques such as particle size reduction, solid dispersions, or the use of solubilizing agents to enhance dissolution. Dissolution testing under simulated gastrointestinal conditions is critical for verifying that the drug is released in a manner comparable to the RLD.

5. **Stability Considerations**
The formulation must remain stable under storage conditions specified for the product's shelf life. Stability studies involve evaluating the drug under conditions of temperature, humidity, and light to identify any potential degradation pathways. Stabilizing agents, such as antioxidants or pH adjusters, may be incorporated to prevent degradation.

6. **Robust Manufacturing Process**
The formulation design must consider scalability and reproducibility during manufacturing. Parameters like mixing, granulation, and compression are optimized to ensure that the product retains uniformity and quality across large production batches.

7. **Compliance with Regulatory Guidelines**
The formulation must adhere to regulatory requirements for pharmaceutical equivalence, bioequivalence, and labeling. For example, the FDA's guidance on inactive ingredients ensures that any excipient differences do not impact safety or efficacy.

Challenges and Solutions in Formulation Design

1. **Complex Dosage Forms**
For formulations such as controlled-release systems or transdermal patches, replicating the RLD's release profile is challenging. Advanced techniques like matrix systems or coated pellets are often employed to

achieve equivalent release characteristics.

2. **Low Solubility Drugs**

   Poorly soluble drugs require innovative solutions like nanoformulations or the use of surfactants to enhance bioavailability. Preformulation studies guide these modifications.

3. **Taste Masking**

   For oral formulations, especially in pediatric products, ensuring palatability is crucial. Techniques like coating or the use of flavoring agents are incorporated while maintaining bioequivalence.

4. **Excipients Interactions**

   Excipient compatibility studies minimize risks of interactions that could compromise stability or performance. For example, avoiding reactive excipients or adjusting proportions can mitigate issues.

Case Example

Consider a generic version of a controlled-release antihypertensive drug. The RLD uses a polymer matrix to achieve sustained release over 12 hours. The generic formulation incorporates a similar polymer system, verified through in vitro dissolution studies and bioequivalence testing, ensuring the drug release matches the RLD's profile. Additional excipients are selected to maintain stability and manufacturability, resulting in a bioequivalent and stable product.

6.2 Optimization of Formulation Composition

Optimization of formulation composition is a critical phase in the development of generic drug products. This process involves refining the formulation to ensure it meets the desired quality, safety, and efficacy standards while achieving bioequivalence with the reference listed drug. Advanced scientific approaches, such as Design of Experiments (DoE) and Quality by Design (QbD), are commonly used to systematically optimize dosage forms. These approaches allow developers to explore multiple formulation variables simultaneously, identify critical quality attributes, and establish robust manufacturing processes.

Approaches to Optimize Dosage Forms

1. **Design of Experiments (DoE)**

   DoE is a systematic approach to studying the relationships between formulation variables and their effects on product performance. Instead of altering one variable at a time, DoE evaluates multiple factors simultaneously, leading to a deeper understanding of how these factors interact.

- **Steps in DoE for Formulation Optimization:**

  - Identify **critical factors**: Variables such as excipient type, concentration, mixing time, and particle size.
  - Define **response variables**: Outcomes like dissolution rate, tablet hardness, or drug release profile.
  - Create an **experimental design**: Common designs include factorial designs, response surface methodology (RSM), and mixture designs.
  - Analyze results: Statistical tools such as regression analysis and contour plots are used to identify optimal conditions.

- **Example**: In optimizing a sustained-release tablet, DoE can help determine the ideal polymer concentration and compression force to achieve the desired drug release profile over 12 hours.

2. **Quality by Design (QbD)**
   QbD is a regulatory-driven framework that emphasizes a systematic understanding of the product and process to ensure consistent quality. It involves defining quality attributes early in development and designing the formulation to meet these attributes reliably.

   - **Key Elements of QbD in Formulation Optimization:**

     - Define the **Quality Target Product Profile (QTPP)**: Characteristics such as dissolution, bioavailability, and stability.
     - Identify **Critical Quality Attributes (CQAs)**: Properties that impact the product's performance, like drug particle size or excipient compatibility.
     - Conduct **risk assessment**: Tools like Failure Mode and Effects Analysis (FMEA) identify high-risk variables.
     - Develop a **control strategy**: Establish parameters and monitoring systems to maintain quality during manufacturing.

- **Example**: In a liquid formulation, QbD can guide the selection of stabilizers and preservatives to ensure stability without compromising bioavailability.

Applications in Dosage Form Optimization

1. **Solid Oral Dosage Forms**

   - In tablets and capsules, optimization focuses on improving dissolution rates, compressibility, and uniformity. For instance, DoE can determine the optimal binder concentration to balance tablet hardness with disintegration time.
   - QbD ensures the formulation remains stable and performs consistently under varying manufacturing conditions.

2. **Controlled-Release Systems**

   - These formulations require precise optimization of drug release mechanisms. DoE can evaluate the effects of polymer type and coating thickness on the release profile, while QbD ensures robust manufacturing processes.

3. **Parenteral Products**

   - Injections require optimization to maintain sterility, stability, and bioavailability. DoE can help determine the best pH and excipient combination to minimize degradation.

4. **Topical and Transdermal Products**

   - Optimization involves balancing drug permeability and adhesion. For transdermal patches, DoE can evaluate adhesive properties, while QbD ensures reproducibility across production batches.

Advantages of Using DoE and QbD

- **Efficiency**: Reduces the time and cost associated with traditional trial-and-error methods.

- **Comprehensive Understanding**: Identifies interactions between variables that might otherwise be missed.
- **Regulatory Compliance**: Aligns with regulatory expectations for a science-based approach to product development.
- **Enhanced Product Quality**: Ensures the formulation is robust and less susceptible to variations in manufacturing conditions.

Case Example

In developing a generic sustained-release formulation of metformin, DoE was used to optimize the polymer concentration and compression force. The experiments revealed that a 20% polymer concentration and moderate compression force provided the desired 12-hour release profile. Simultaneously, QbD principles guided the risk assessment and control strategy, ensuring consistent performance across production batches.

6.3 Process Development and Scale-up

Process development and scale-up are critical steps in the transition from laboratory-scale formulation development to full-scale manufacturing. The goal of scaling up is to replicate the formulation and process parameters established during laboratory development on a larger production scale while ensuring that the product maintains its quality, safety, and efficacy. This step is essential for translating the optimized formulation into a consistent, reproducible, and economically viable product that meets regulatory standards.

Importance of Scaling Formulations from Lab to Production

1. **Consistency and Reproducibility**

   Scaling up ensures that the product retains its critical quality attributes, such as dissolution rate, stability, and bioavailability, across all production batches. Processes optimized at the lab scale may behave differently during production due to changes in equipment size, material handling, and environmental factors. Process development identifies these differences and adjusts parameters to achieve uniformity.

2. **Understanding Process Parameters**

   During scale-up, it is crucial to define and optimize key process parameters that influence product quality. These parameters include mixing time, granulation speed, drying temperature, and compression force. For example, in tablet manufacturing, variations in compression force during scale-up can impact tablet hardness and disintegration time.

Identifying the acceptable operating range for these parameters ensures product consistency.

3. **Equipment Selection and Process Transfer**

   Laboratory equipment often differs significantly from production-scale machinery. The scale-up process evaluates the impact of equipment differences on product performance. For instance, the mixing efficiency of a small-scale blender may not directly translate to a large industrial mixer, requiring adjustments in mixing time or speed. Process transfer documentation ensures seamless replication of the manufacturing process in a production environment.

4. **Validation and Regulatory Compliance**

   Scale-up activities include process validation to demonstrate that the manufacturing process consistently produces a product that meets predefined quality specifications. Validation studies include three consecutive, reproducible batches under specified conditions. Regulatory agencies, such as the FDA, require detailed documentation of scale-up and validation processes to ensure compliance with Good Manufacturing Practices (GMP).

5. **Economic Feasibility**

   Large-scale production must be cost-effective while maintaining product quality. Scale-up activities optimize resource utilization, minimize waste, and streamline manufacturing processes to reduce costs without compromising quality. For example, efficient material flow and process design can significantly lower production expenses.

6. **Challenges in Scale-up**

   - **Process Variability**: Differences in equipment size, heat transfer, and mixing dynamics can introduce variability. For instance, in wet granulation, larger equipment may result in uneven distribution of binder, affecting granule size and quality.
   - **Material Behavior**: Materials may exhibit different flow properties or compaction behaviors at scale. For example, fine powders may cause segregation during handling, requiring adjustments in excipient ratios or granulation techniques.
   - **Environmental Factors**: Humidity, temperature, and airflow differences in production facilities can impact product stability and performance.

- ○ **Quality Control Challenges**: Increased batch sizes demand more rigorous in-process testing to ensure compliance with quality standards.

7. **Case Example**

Consider a generic sustained-release formulation of an antihypertensive drug. At the laboratory scale, the formulation achieved the desired release profile using a small-scale fluid bed granulator. During scale-up, inconsistencies in granule size were observed due to differences in airflow patterns and spray rates in larger equipment. Process development adjusted the spray rate and granulation time, ensuring consistent granule size and drug release across production batches.

8. **Pilot-Scale and Commercial-Scale Testing**

Pilot-scale studies serve as an intermediate step between lab and full-scale production. They allow manufacturers to refine process parameters and address scale-up challenges before transitioning to commercial-scale manufacturing. These studies validate the feasibility of the process and highlight any required adjustments.

CHAPTER SEVEN

Process Development and Optimization

7.1 Manufacturing Process Design

Manufacturing process design is a crucial aspect of drug development, ensuring that the product is produced consistently, safely, and efficiently. The design process involves translating the laboratory-scale formulation into a scalable, reproducible manufacturing process. It requires careful consideration of both scientific and practical aspects to achieve quality and compliance with regulatory standards. Key considerations for process development include understanding the product's characteristics, selecting appropriate equipment, optimizing process parameters, and ensuring compliance with Good Manufacturing Practices (GMP).

Considerations for Process Development

1. **Understanding Product Characteristics**

   - The physical and chemical properties of the drug substance and excipients significantly influence process design. Factors such as particle size, solubility, polymorphism, and stability must be considered to ensure the process maintains the product's critical quality attributes.
   - For example, a highly hygroscopic drug may require controlled humidity conditions during processing to prevent degradation.

2. **Process Selection and Scalability**

   - The chosen manufacturing process must be scalable from laboratory to commercial production.

- Common processes include direct compression for tablets, wet granulation for improved flow properties, and extrusion for controlled-release formulations.
- Scalability challenges, such as differences in mixing efficiency or drying rates between small-scale and large-scale equipment, must be addressed during process design.

3. **Equipment Compatibility**

- The selection of equipment plays a vital role in ensuring process consistency and efficiency. The equipment must be compatible with the formulation's properties and capable of maintaining product quality during production.
- For instance, high-shear mixers may be preferred for wet granulation, while fluid bed dryers are used for efficient drying of granules.

4. **Critical Process Parameters (CPPs)**

- Identifying and controlling critical process parameters is essential for maintaining product quality. CPPs include variables such as mixing time, compression force, granulation temperature, and drying time.
- These parameters are optimized through pilot-scale studies and validated to ensure they remain within acceptable ranges during production.

5. **Quality by Design (QbD) Approach**

- Implementing a QbD framework helps in systematically understanding and controlling the manufacturing process.
- QbD identifies critical quality attributes (CQAs) of the product and ensures that the process consistently meets these attributes through risk assessment and design of experiments.

6. **In-Process Controls (IPCs)**

- In-process controls are implemented to monitor and adjust critical parameters in real-time. For example, measuring tablet weight, hardness, and disintegration time during production ensures consistency in batch quality.

- IPCs reduce variability and minimize the risk of batch failures.

7. Process Validation

- Validation ensures that the manufacturing process consistently produces a product meeting predefined specifications.
- It involves three consecutive, reproducible batches and extensive documentation of the process parameters and quality outcomes.
- Regulatory agencies require detailed validation reports to confirm compliance with GMP standards.

8. Environmental and Safety Considerations

- Process design must address environmental factors, such as temperature, humidity, and air quality, to prevent product degradation or contamination.
- Safety measures, including dust control systems and proper handling of hazardous materials, ensure worker and product safety during manufacturing.

9. Economic Feasibility

- The process must be cost-effective while maintaining product quality. Efficient material utilization, minimal waste, and optimized cycle times contribute to economic feasibility.
- For instance, continuous manufacturing processes can reduce costs compared to traditional batch processes by improving efficiency and reducing downtime.

10. Regulatory Compliance

- The process design must adhere to regulatory guidelines issued by authorities such as the FDA or EMA.
- Compliance with GMP and submission of detailed process descriptions in the drug application are mandatory to obtain approval for commercialization.

Example

Consider the development of a film-coated tablet for a generic pain reliever. The process design involves selecting direct compression for its simplicity and efficiency. Critical parameters, such as blending time and compression force, are optimized during pilot studies. A coating process is added to ensure taste masking and stability, with in-process controls monitoring coating uniformity and drying times. Validation ensures reproducibility, and environmental controls are implemented to manage humidity, as the active ingredient is hygroscopic.

7.3 Critical Process Parameters (CPP) and Critical Quality Attributes (CQA)

Critical Process Parameters (CPP) and Critical Quality Attributes (CQA) are integral components of process development in pharmaceutical manufacturing. Their identification, understanding, and monitoring ensure that the product meets predefined quality standards while maintaining safety and efficacy. CPPs are the process variables that significantly impact CQAs, which are the measurable properties that define the product's quality. By systematically identifying and controlling CPPs and CQAs during development, manufacturers can achieve consistency and compliance with regulatory requirements.

Understanding Critical Quality Attributes (CQA)

Critical Quality Attributes are physical, chemical, biological, or microbiological properties that must be controlled to ensure the product meets its intended quality and performance. CQAs are identified based on their potential impact on the product's safety, efficacy, and patient acceptability.

- **Examples of CQAs:**

  - For tablets: Uniformity of dosage, hardness, disintegration time, and dissolution profile.
  - For injectables: Sterility, pH, particulate matter, and stability.
  - For transdermal systems: Adhesion strength, drug release rate, and patch uniformity.

- **CQA Identification:**

- ◦ CQAs are determined during preformulation and formulation studies, where the product's critical characteristics are evaluated.
- ◦ Risk assessment tools such as Failure Mode and Effects Analysis (FMEA) are used to prioritize CQAs based on their potential impact.

- **Significance:**

  - ◦ Controlling CQAs ensures the product consistently delivers its intended therapeutic effect and complies with regulatory guidelines.

Understanding Critical Process Parameters (CPP)

Critical Process Parameters are variables within the manufacturing process that must be controlled to ensure CQAs remain within acceptable limits. Variability in CPPs can directly affect the quality and consistency of the final product.

- **Examples of CPPs:**

  - ◦ In tablet manufacturing: Granulation time, blending speed, compression force, and coating temperature.
  - ◦ In injectables: Sterilization temperature, filtration rate, and mixing speed.
  - ◦ In transdermal systems: Casting speed, drying temperature, and adhesive thickness.

- **CPP Identification:**

  - ◦ CPPs are identified using scientific and statistical methods, such as Design of Experiments (DoE).
  - ◦ Pilot-scale studies and process optimization activities highlight parameters that significantly influence CQAs.

- **Significance:**

  - ◦ Maintaining CPPs within defined ranges ensures reproducibility and prevents batch failures.

Monitoring CPPs and CQAs During Development

1. **Process Understanding:**

   - Comprehensive understanding of the product and process is established during development. This involves studying the relationships between CPPs and CQAs through DoE and risk assessments.

2. **Process Analytical Technology (PAT):**

   - PAT tools enable real-time monitoring and control of CPPs to ensure CQAs are consistently achieved.
   - For example, near-infrared spectroscopy (NIR) can monitor blend uniformity in real time during tablet manufacturing.

3. **In-Process Controls (IPCs):**

   - IPCs are implemented to measure CPPs at critical stages of production. This ensures that process deviations are detected early, preventing quality issues.
   - Examples include hardness testing for tablets during compression or monitoring temperature during sterilization.

4. **Validation:**

   - Process validation confirms that CPPs and CQAs are consistently controlled across production batches. Validation involves three consecutive successful batches produced under defined conditions.

5. **Control Strategy:**

   - A control strategy integrates monitoring systems and corrective actions to maintain CPPs and CQAs within acceptable ranges. This strategy is documented in regulatory submissions to demonstrate compliance.

Example

In the development of an extended-release tablet, dissolution profile is a critical quality attribute that ensures the drug releases at the intended rate. Granulation time and polymer concentration are identified as critical process parameters influencing the dissolution profile. During development, granulation time is optimized through DoE to balance drug release and tablet hardness. In-process controls monitor polymer dispersion to prevent variability in drug release. Validation ensures reproducibility, and PAT tools provide real-time data on granulation consistency.

CHAPTER EIGHT

Analytical Method Development and Validation

8.1 Introduction to Analytical Methods

Analytical methods are essential tools in pharmaceutical development, enabling precise measurement and evaluation of drug substances, formulations, and finished products. Developing reliable analytical methods ensures that all components meet quality standards and regulatory requirements, safeguarding patient safety and product efficacy. These methods are used throughout the drug development lifecycle, from preformulation to manufacturing, ensuring consistency, accuracy, and compliance.

Importance of Developing Reliable Analytical Methods

Reliable analytical methods are vital for assessing the physical, chemical, and microbiological characteristics of drug substances and products. Their importance lies in the following aspects:

1. **Ensuring Product Quality**

   Analytical methods verify that the product meets defined specifications for identity, potency, purity, and stability. For example, high-performance liquid chromatography (HPLC) is commonly used to quantify the active ingredient and detect impurities in drug formulations. By ensuring product quality, these methods build confidence in the safety and efficacy of medications.

2. **Supporting Regulatory Compliance**

   Regulatory agencies like the FDA and EMA require robust analytical data for drug approval. Analytical methods must adhere to guidelines such as those outlined by the International Council for Harmonisation (ICH) for validation. Reliable methods ensure that the product complies with regulatory expectations for quality and consistency.

3. **Monitoring Process Parameters**

Analytical methods are used to monitor critical process parameters during manufacturing. For instance, real-time monitoring of blend uniformity in tablet production ensures consistency across batches. These methods help identify and rectify deviations early, reducing the risk of batch failures.

4. **Detecting and Controlling Impurities**

Impurities in drug substances can compromise safety and efficacy. Analytical methods, such as gas chromatography (GC) or mass spectrometry (MS), are used to identify and quantify impurities. This ensures that the drug meets regulatory limits for residual solvents, degradation products, and other impurities.

5. **Evaluating Stability**

Stability studies rely on analytical methods to measure changes in the drug's potency, purity, or appearance under various environmental conditions. For example, UV spectroscopy can be used to monitor the degradation of a photosensitive drug. These studies establish the product's shelf life and storage conditions.

6. **Facilitating Generic Drug Development**

In generic drug development, analytical methods are crucial for demonstrating bioequivalence to the reference listed drug. Methods must provide accurate data on dissolution rates, impurity profiles, and other quality attributes to support Abbreviated New Drug Application (ANDA) submissions.

7. **Cost and Time Efficiency**

Reliable analytical methods reduce the time and cost of product development by providing accurate data quickly and minimizing the need for repeated testing. Automated methods, such as robotic sample preparation or online monitoring systems, further enhance efficiency.

Example

Consider a generic tablet containing atorvastatin. During its development, HPLC is used to quantify atorvastatin and identify potential degradation products under stress conditions. Dissolution testing is conducted to compare the release profile of the generic with the reference listed drug. By employing validated methods, developers ensure the product meets bioequivalence and stability requirements, supporting regulatory approval.

8.2 Analytical Method Development for API and Excipients

Analytical method development for active pharmaceutical ingredients (APIs) and excipients is a crucial step in ensuring the quality, safety, and efficacy of pharmaceutical products. These methods enable accurate identification, quantification, and characterization of both APIs and excipients. Developing robust and reproducible testing techniques ensures compliance with regulatory standards and supports the reliable manufacturing of consistent drug products.

Techniques for Developing Testing Methods

1. **High-Performance Liquid Chromatography (HPLC)**

   - HPLC is one of the most commonly used techniques for developing analytical methods for APIs and excipients.
   - It separates compounds based on their interaction with the stationary and mobile phases. This technique is highly sensitive and can detect impurities and degradation products.
   - Parameters optimized during HPLC method development include:

     - Selection of column type (e.g., C18 or C8).
     - Mobile phase composition (e.g., water/acetonitrile gradient).
     - Flow rate and detection wavelength.

   - Example: Determining the assay and impurity profile of an API such as ibuprofen.

2. **Gas Chromatography (GC)**

   - GC is widely used for analyzing volatile and semi-volatile compounds, including residual solvents in APIs and excipients.
   - Development involves selecting an appropriate column and optimizing parameters like carrier gas flow and oven temperature gradient.
   - Example: Quantifying ethanol as a residual solvent in lactose used as an excipient.

3. **Ultraviolet-Visible Spectroscopy (UV-Vis)**

- UV-Vis spectroscopy is a simple and cost-effective technique for identifying and quantifying compounds that absorb light in the UV or visible range.
- Method development includes determining the wavelength of maximum absorption (λmax) and establishing a calibration curve.
- Example: Measuring the concentration of an API like paracetamol in solution.

4. Fourier Transform Infrared Spectroscopy (FTIR)

- FTIR is used for qualitative identification of functional groups in APIs and excipients.
- Development involves scanning the sample and comparing the spectrum to reference standards.
- Example: Confirming the identity of an excipient like microcrystalline cellulose.

5. Titration Techniques

- Classical titration methods are still relevant for certain APIs and excipients, particularly for determining content uniformity and stability.
- Examples include acid-base titrations for APIs like acetylsalicylic acid or complexometric titrations for excipients containing metal ions.

6. Mass Spectrometry (MS)

- MS is employed for highly accurate identification of compounds based on their mass-to-charge ratio.
- Coupled with techniques like HPLC or GC, MS can detect trace impurities and degradation products.
- Example: Identifying impurities in an API with low molecular weight.

7. Dissolution Testing

- Dissolution testing is critical for APIs and formulations containing excipients that influence drug release.

- Method development involves selecting dissolution media, agitation speeds, and temperature.
- Example: Assessing the dissolution rate of an extended-release tablet formulation.

8. X-Ray Diffraction (XRD)

- XRD is used for characterizing the crystalline structure of APIs and excipients.
- It helps identify polymorphs and assess the compatibility between APIs and excipients.
- Example: Determining the polymorphic form of an API to ensure batch-to-batch consistency.

9. Thermal Analysis (DSC and TGA)

- Differential Scanning Calorimetry (DSC) and Thermogravimetric Analysis (TGA) are used for studying the thermal properties of APIs and excipients.
- These techniques help in understanding melting points, phase transitions, and degradation temperatures.
- Example: Evaluating the compatibility of an API with a polymer excipient used in a controlled-release formulation.

Key Steps in Method Development

1. Defining the Purpose of the Method

- Clearly outline the method's objectives, such as impurity detection, content uniformity, or dissolution profiling.
- For example, the method for quantifying an API in bulk powder may differ from that for a finished product.

2. Choosing the Analytical Technique

- Select the appropriate technique based on the properties of the API or excipient and the method's objectives.

- For instance, volatile impurities require GC, while non-volatile compounds may be better analyzed using HPLC.

3. Developing Analytical Parameters

- Optimize parameters specific to the technique, such as wavelength for UV-Vis, column selection for HPLC, or carrier gas for GC.

4. Validation of the Method

- Validate the developed method according to International Council for Harmonisation (ICH) guidelines, covering parameters such as accuracy, precision, linearity, range, specificity, and robustness.
- For example, an HPLC method for an API must demonstrate accuracy within ±2% and a relative standard deviation (RSD) of less than 2% for repeatability.

Example Application

In the development of a generic drug containing metformin, HPLC is used to quantify metformin content and detect degradation products under stress conditions. UV-Vis spectroscopy verifies the presence of excipients like povidone, while FTIR confirms their identity. Dissolution testing ensures that the excipients do not affect the API's release rate compared to the reference listed drug.

8.3 Validation of Analytical Methods

Validation of analytical methods is a critical process in pharmaceutical development that ensures the reliability, consistency, and accuracy of the methods used for testing drug substances, drug products, and excipients. Regulatory agencies such as the FDA and the EMA require validated methods to confirm that analytical procedures meet the intended purpose and produce reproducible results under specified conditions. This process is guided by regulatory standards, such as the International Council for Harmonisation (ICH) guidelines Q2(R1), which outline the key parameters and requirements for validation.

Steps in Method Validation

1. Define the Purpose and Scope

- Clearly outline the method's intended purpose, such as identifying impurities, quantifying the active ingredient, or verifying dissolution rates.
- Specify the sample type, test conditions, and acceptance criteria.

2. **Select Validation Parameters**

- The following parameters are typically validated, depending on the method's purpose:

  - Accuracy
  - Precision
  - Specificity
  - Linearity
  - Range
  - Limit of detection (LOD)
  - Limit of quantitation (LOQ)
  - Robustness
  - System suitability

3. **Accuracy Testing**

- Accuracy measures how close the test results are to the true value.
- Performed by spiking known amounts of the analyte into the sample matrix and comparing the results.
- Acceptance criteria: Recovery within 98-102% of the true value.

4. **Precision Testing**

- Precision evaluates the repeatability and reproducibility of the method.
- Includes:

  - Repeatability: Same analyst, same equipment, and same day.
  - Intermediate precision: Different analysts, equipment, and days.

- Acceptance criteria: Relative standard deviation (RSD) less than 2%.

5. **Specificity**

   - Specificity ensures the method can differentiate the analyte from other components, such as impurities, excipients, and degradation products.
   - Assessed using samples containing potential interferences.

6. **Linearity**

   - Linearity assesses the method's ability to produce results directly proportional to the analyte concentration within a specified range.
   - Typically evaluated across five concentration levels.
   - Acceptance criteria: Correlation coefficient (R^2) ≥ 0.99.

7. **Range**

   - Range defines the interval between the lowest and highest concentrations that can be accurately and precisely measured.
   - Determined based on the method's intended application, such as content uniformity or assay testing.

8. **LOD and LOQ**

   - Limit of detection (LOD): The smallest amount of analyte detectable but not quantifiable.
   - Limit of quantitation (LOQ): The smallest amount of analyte that can be quantified with accuracy and precision.
   - Calculated using signal-to-noise ratios of 3:1 (LOD) and 10:1 (LOQ).

9. **Robustness**

   - Robustness evaluates the method's ability to remain unaffected by small changes in experimental conditions, such as pH, temperature, or flow rate.
   - Variations in these parameters are introduced to assess the method's reliability.

10. **System Suitability Testing**

- System suitability ensures that the analytical system is performing as expected before sample analysis.
- Parameters such as peak resolution, tailing factor, and theoretical plates are evaluated.
- Example criteria: Resolution > 2.0, tailing factor < 1.5, theoretical plates > 2000.

Regulatory Requirements for Validation

1. **ICH Guidelines**

- ICH Q2(R1) provides comprehensive guidelines on validation parameters for analytical methods, covering accuracy, precision, specificity, and robustness.
- Methods must be validated for their intended use in routine quality control or stability testing.

2. **Good Laboratory Practices (GLP)**

- All validation studies must adhere to GLP to ensure data integrity and reproducibility.

3. **Documentation**

- Validation results must be thoroughly documented, including experimental conditions, data, calculations, and conclusions.
- Validation reports should include:

  - Objective and scope of validation.
  - Method description.
  - Validation results with supporting data.
  - Acceptance criteria and conclusions.

4. **Revalidation**

- Methods must be revalidated when significant changes are made to the formulation, manufacturing process, or analytical method.

- ○ Examples include changes in API source, excipient grade, or test equipment.

5. **Submission to Regulatory Agencies**

- ○ For drug approval, validated methods must be included in regulatory submissions, such as the New Drug Application (NDA) or Abbreviated New Drug Application (ANDA).
- ○ Regulatory agencies may review validation data during inspections or dossier evaluations.

Example of Method Validation

For a generic paracetamol tablet, HPLC is used to quantify the active ingredient and detect impurities.

- Accuracy: Recovery within 98-102% across three concentration levels.
- Precision: RSD < 2% for six replicate injections.
- Specificity: Ability to separate paracetamol from its degradation products and excipients.
- Linearity: R^2 = 0.999 over the range of 10-150% of the target concentration.
- Robustness: Consistent results under slight variations in flow rate and column temperature.

CHAPTER NINE

Stability Studies for Generic Products

9.1 Stability Testing for APIs

Stability testing is a critical component of drug development, aimed at determining how the quality of an active pharmaceutical ingredient (API) varies with time under the influence of environmental factors such as temperature, humidity, and light. For APIs, stability testing helps establish appropriate storage conditions, shelf life, and retest intervals, ensuring that the drug substance maintains its potency, purity, and safety throughout its intended use. Regulatory agencies such as the FDA, EMA, and ICH provide detailed guidelines for conducting stability studies.

Purpose of Stability Testing for APIs

1. **Determine Degradation Pathways:**
   Stability testing identifies the chemical, physical, and microbiological degradation pathways of the API, including hydrolysis, oxidation, and photodegradation.

2. **Establish Storage Conditions:**
   Results from stability testing help define optimal storage conditions, such as temperature and humidity, to maintain the API's integrity.

3. **Assign Retest Periods:**
   Stability studies determine the timeframe within which the API can be retested and used in manufacturing, ensuring compliance with quality standards.

4. **Support Regulatory Submissions:**
   Stability data are a mandatory part of regulatory submissions, including Drug Master Files (DMFs) and product dossiers.

Types of Stability Testing

1. **Stress Testing (Forced Degradation Studies):**

   - Conducted to identify potential degradation pathways by subjecting the API to extreme conditions such as high temperatures, UV light, acidic and alkaline solutions, and oxidative environments.
   - Example: Hydrochloric acid stress tests reveal API sensitivity to acidic conditions.

2. **Accelerated Stability Testing:**

   - Carried out under elevated temperature and humidity conditions, typically 40°C ± 2°C and 75% RH ± 5%.
   - Designed to predict long-term stability in a shorter time.
   - Example: A three-month study simulates the behavior of an API over two years of real-time storage.

3. **Long-Term Stability Testing:**

   - Conducted under controlled conditions representing actual storage environments, such as 25°C ± 2°C and 60% RH ± 5%.
   - Provides data to establish retest intervals and shelf life.

4. **Intermediate Stability Testing:**

   - Performed under conditions such as 30°C ± 2°C and 65% RH ± 5% to evaluate stability in regions with intermediate climatic conditions.

Key Parameters Monitored During Stability Testing

1. **Assay:**

   - Quantification of the API's potency over time to ensure it remains within acceptable limits, typically ±5% of the initial value.

2. **Impurity Profile:**

- Monitoring degradation products to ensure they do not exceed regulatory thresholds, such as 0.5% for most APIs unless otherwise specified.

3. **Physical Properties:**

   - Evaluation of attributes like color, odor, and crystallinity, which may indicate degradation.

4. **Moisture Content:**

   - Measured using techniques like Karl Fischer titration, as excessive moisture can accelerate degradation.

5. **pH:**

   - For APIs in solution, pH stability ensures compatibility with formulation requirements.

6. **Microbial Contamination:**

   - Ensures that APIs susceptible to microbiological degradation meet sterility or microbial limit requirements.

Analytical Techniques Used

1. **High-Performance Liquid Chromatography (HPLC):**

   - Commonly used for quantifying the API and identifying degradation products.
   - Example: Separating and quantifying oxidized impurities in a beta-lactam antibiotic.

2. **Gas Chromatography (GC):**

   - Suitable for volatile compounds and residual solvent analysis.

3. **Fourier-Transform Infrared Spectroscopy (FTIR):**

- ◦ Used to detect changes in functional groups indicative of chemical degradation.

4. **Differential Scanning Calorimetry (DSC):**

   - ◦ Measures changes in thermal properties like melting point, which can indicate polymorphic transitions.

5. **X-Ray Diffraction (XRD):**

   - ◦ Identifies changes in crystalline structure that could affect stability.

Regulatory Guidelines for Stability Testing

1. **ICH Guidelines:**

   - ◦ ICH Q1A provides comprehensive guidance on stability testing, including protocols for accelerated, long-term, and intermediate studies.

2. **FDA and EMA Requirements:**

   - ◦ Emphasize the inclusion of stability data in DMFs and regulatory filings.
   - ◦ APIs used in regions with different climatic zones must meet specific stability requirements for those regions.

3. **Documentation:**

   - ◦ Stability protocols, raw data, and summary reports must be included in regulatory submissions.
   - ◦ Example: A Certificate of Analysis (CoA) detailing stability results over defined intervals.

Example Application

In the development of a generic antiviral API, stability testing revealed sensitivity to moisture, leading to hydrolytic degradation. Based on the findings, the API was stored in airtight, desiccated containers, and magnesium stearate was avoided as a moisture-absorbing excipient during formulation. The retest period was established as two years under 25°C and 60% RH.

Factors Affecting API Stability

The stability of an active pharmaceutical ingredient (API) can be influenced by various physical, chemical, and environmental factors. Identifying and understanding these factors are critical for ensuring the quality, efficacy, and safety of the drug product throughout its shelf life. Below are the key factors affecting API stability:

1. Environmental Factors

- **Temperature:**
  Elevated temperatures can accelerate chemical reactions such as oxidation, hydrolysis, and degradation. For example, antibiotics like penicillins are highly temperature-sensitive and degrade quickly under high heat.
- **Humidity:**
  APIs that are hygroscopic (absorb moisture) can degrade via hydrolysis in humid environments. Moisture can also promote microbial growth or induce physical changes like clumping in powders.
- **Light (Photostability):**
  APIs sensitive to light, such as ascorbic acid or nifedipine, may undergo photodegradation, leading to loss of potency or formation of harmful degradation products.
- **Oxygen (Oxidative Stability):**
  APIs exposed to air may oxidize, resulting in reduced efficacy. For instance, catecholamines like epinephrine are highly prone to oxidation.

2. Chemical Factors

- **Hydrolysis:**
  The reaction of APIs with water, especially in solution or humid conditions, can cause significant degradation. Esters, amides, and lactones are particularly susceptible.
- **Oxidation:**
  Oxidative degradation occurs due to exposure to oxygen or reactive oxidative species. APIs containing phenolic or unsaturated groups are particularly vulnerable.

- **pH Sensitivity:**
APIs may degrade more rapidly in certain pH environments. For example, weak acids and bases may degrade at extreme acidic or basic pH values.
- **Polymorphic Stability:**
Polymorphic changes (transition between crystalline forms) can affect the solubility and stability of the API. For example, polymorphs of ritonavir exhibit varied stability profiles.

3. Physical Factors

- **Particle Size:**
Smaller particles have a larger surface area exposed to environmental factors, making them more susceptible to degradation.
- **Crystallinity:**
Amorphous forms of APIs may exhibit higher solubility but are often less stable than their crystalline counterparts.
- **Excipients and Formulation Matrix:**
Interactions between APIs and excipients, such as magnesium stearate or lactose, can lead to degradation. Compatibility studies are essential to mitigate these risks.

4. Storage and Packaging

- **Packaging Material:**
Inadequate packaging, such as permeable plastic containers, can expose APIs to moisture, light, or oxygen, accelerating degradation.
- **Storage Conditions:**
APIs stored in suboptimal conditions, such as extreme temperatures or high humidity, can degrade more rapidly.

ICH Guidelines for Stability Testing

The **International Council for Harmonisation (ICH)** has established comprehensive guidelines for conducting stability studies to ensure drug substances and products maintain their quality over time. Key ICH guidelines include:

1. ICH Q1A (R2): Stability Testing of New Drug Substances and Products

- **Scope:**
This guideline provides recommendations for testing APIs and drug products under specific environmental conditions to determine their shelf life and storage conditions.
- **Storage Conditions and Testing:**

  - Long-term testing: 25°C ± 2°C, 60% RH ± 5%, conducted for at least 12 months.
  - Accelerated testing: 40°C ± 2°C, 75% RH ± 5%, conducted for at least 6 months.
  - Intermediate testing (if required): 30°C ± 2°C, 65% RH ± 5%, for products sensitive to high humidity or temperature.

- **Frequency of Testing:**

  - Initial, 3, 6, 9, and 12 months for accelerated and long-term conditions.
  - At least every 3 months in the first year and annually thereafter for long-term studies.

2. ICH Q1B: Photostability Testing

- **Scope:**
Photostability testing evaluates the effects of light exposure on the API or drug product.
- **Testing Conditions:**

  - Samples are exposed to UV and visible light to simulate the effects of sunlight and indoor lighting.
  - The sample is compared to a protected control to assess changes in potency, color, or impurity levels.

3. ICH Q1C: Stability Testing for New Dosage Forms

- **Scope:**
Provides guidelines for stability studies specific to new dosage forms of existing APIs.
- **Key Requirements:**

- ◦ Similar conditions as Q1A but tailored to the specific characteristics of the new dosage form.

4. ICH Q1D: Bracketing and Matrixing

- **Scope:**
  Offers guidelines for reducing the number of stability samples by testing at the extremes of design (bracketing) or at a representative subset (matrixing).

5. ICH Q1E: Evaluation of Stability Data

- **Scope:**
  Provides recommendations for analyzing stability data and determining the shelf life and retest intervals.
- **Key Considerations:**

  - ◦ Statistical analysis to confirm trends in potency, impurity levels, and other critical parameters.
  - ◦ Justification for extrapolating shelf life beyond the data period.

6. ICH Q1F: Stability Data for Climatic Zones III and IV

- **Scope:**
  Addresses stability testing for regions with hot and humid climates.
- **Conditions:**

  - ◦ Zone III: 30°C ± 2°C, 35% RH ± 5%.
  - ◦ Zone IVa: 30°C ± 2°C, 65% RH ± 5%.
  - ◦ Zone IVb: 30°C ± 2°C, 75% RH ± 5%.

9.2 Stability Testing for Finished Dosage Forms

Stability testing for finished dosage forms is a critical process in pharmaceutical development and manufacturing. It ensures that the drug product maintains its intended quality, safety, and efficacy throughout its shelf life under recommended storage conditions. These studies assess how factors such as environmental conditions, packaging, and formulation components affect the stability of the final product. Adhering to stability testing guidelines provided by regulatory agencies like the ICH is mandatory for obtaining product approval and market authorization.

Purpose of Stability Testing for Finished Dosage Forms

1. **Evaluate Product Integrity:**
   Stability testing verifies that the physical, chemical, and microbiological properties of the dosage form remain within predefined specifications.
2. **Determine Shelf Life:**
   The data generated establishes the product's expiration date and recommended storage conditions.
3. **Assess Packaging Compatibility:**
   Stability studies ensure that the packaging protects the product from environmental factors and does not interact with the formulation.
4. **Support Regulatory Submissions:**
   Stability data must be included in applications for marketing authorization to demonstrate product reliability over time.

Types of Stability Testing

1. **Real-Time (Long-Term) Stability Testing:**

   - Conducted under normal storage conditions to simulate real-world storage environments.
   - Conditions: **25°C ± 2°C, 60% RH ± 5%** for at least 12 months (or up to the full shelf life).
   - Purpose: Provides definitive data on the product's stability throughout its intended shelf life.

2. **Accelerated Stability Testing:**

   - Conducted at elevated temperature and humidity to predict long-term stability in a shorter timeframe.
   - Conditions: **40°C ± 2°C, 75% RH ± 5%** for at least 6 months.
   - Purpose: Identifies potential degradation pathways and helps determine tentative shelf life.

3. **Intermediate Stability Testing:**

- Performed for products sensitive to high humidity or temperature.
- Conditions: **30°C ± 2°C, 65% RH ± 5%** for at least 6 months.
- Purpose: Assesses stability in regions with intermediate climatic conditions.

4. **Stress Testing:**

- Subjects the product to extreme conditions, such as high temperature, light, and moisture.
- Purpose: Identifies potential degradation products and pathways.

Key Parameters Monitored

1. **Assay:**

- Measures the active ingredient's potency to ensure it remains within acceptable limits (typically 90-110% of the labeled claim).

2. **Impurity Levels:**

- Monitors degradation products to ensure they do not exceed regulatory thresholds.

3. **Dissolution Profile:**

- Ensures the drug release characteristics remain consistent over time.

4. **Physical Characteristics:**

- Monitors changes in appearance, color, odor, texture, and tablet hardness.

5. **Microbial Contamination:**

- Verifies that the product complies with sterility or microbial limits.

6. **Water Content:**

- ◦ Measures moisture levels in solid dosage forms to prevent hydrolysis or clumping.

7. **pH (for Liquid Forms):**

   - ◦ Ensures the pH remains within the specified range to maintain stability and efficacy.

8. **Container-Closure Integrity:**

   - ◦ Assesses the packaging's ability to protect the product from environmental factors like oxygen and moisture.

Analytical Techniques Used

1. **High-Performance Liquid Chromatography (HPLC):**

   - ◦ Used to quantify the active ingredient and detect impurities.

2. **UV-Vis Spectroscopy:**

   - ◦ Suitable for measuring assay and degradation products in liquid formulations.

3. **Dissolution Testing:**

   - ◦ Evaluates the release profile of tablets or capsules over time.

4. **Fourier-Transform Infrared Spectroscopy (FTIR):**

   - ◦ Detects changes in functional groups indicative of degradation.

5. **Microbial Limit Testing:**

   - ◦ Ensures compliance with sterility or microbial contamination standards.

6. **Differential Scanning Calorimetry (DSC):**

○ Monitors thermal properties to detect polymorphic transitions.

Regulatory Guidelines for Stability Testing

1. **ICH Q1A (R2): Stability Testing of New Drug Substances and Products:**

   ○ Provides recommendations for testing finished dosage forms under specified conditions.

2. **ICH Q1B: Photostability Testing:**

   ○ Requires exposure of the product to UV and visible light to assess photostability.

3. **ICH Q1C: Stability Testing for New Dosage Forms:**

   ○ Tailors stability testing protocols to specific dosage forms, such as tablets, capsules, or liquids.

4. **ICH Q1E: Evaluation of Stability Data:**

   ○ Outlines statistical approaches for interpreting stability data and extrapolating shelf life.

5. **ICH Q1F: Stability Data for Climatic Zones III and IV:**

   ○ Specifies testing conditions for hot and humid regions.

Example of Stability Testing
For a generic film-coated tablet containing paracetamol, stability testing would involve:

- Real-time studies at 25°C and 60% RH for 24 months.
- Accelerated testing at 40°C and 75% RH for 6 months.
- Monitoring parameters like assay, dissolution, impurity levels, and tablet hardness.

- Assessing the impact of light exposure on the coating to ensure it protects the drug from degradation.

Protocols for Conducting Stability Studies

A well-defined protocol for stability studies is essential to ensure consistency, accuracy, and compliance with regulatory guidelines. The protocol serves as a blueprint, outlining the procedures, parameters, and conditions under which the stability of an active pharmaceutical ingredient (API) or finished dosage form will be evaluated. Below is a comprehensive framework for designing and implementing stability study protocols.

1. Objective

Clearly state the purpose of the stability study, such as:

- Determining shelf life and expiration dates.
- Identifying suitable storage conditions.
- Evaluating product performance under various environmental factors.

2. Scope

Define the products covered under the protocol, including:

- Active pharmaceutical ingredients.
- Finished dosage forms (tablets, capsules, liquids, injectables).
- Packaging configurations (e.g., blister packs, bottles).

3. Regulatory References

List the guidelines governing the stability study, such as:

- ICH Q1A (R2): Stability Testing of New Drug Substances and Products.
- ICH Q1B: Photostability Testing.
- ICH Q1C: Stability Testing for New Dosage Forms.
- Relevant FDA, EMA, or WHO guidance.

4. Testing Conditions

Specify the storage conditions for stability studies, based on the intended market and product characteristics.

- **Long-Term Testing:**

- ○ Standard conditions: 25°C ± 2°C / 60% RH ± 5%.
- ○ Duration: Typically 12 months to determine the shelf life.

- **Accelerated Testing:**

  - ○ Elevated conditions: 40°C ± 2°C / 75% RH ± 5%.
  - ○ Duration: Minimum of 6 months to predict stability.

- **Intermediate Testing:**

  - ○ Conditions: 30°C ± 2°C / 65% RH ± 5%.
  - ○ Applicable for products sensitive to higher temperatures or humidity.

- **Stress Testing:**

  - ○ Extreme conditions such as high heat (60°C), UV light exposure, high humidity, and oxidation.

- **Photostability Testing:**

  - ○ Expose the product to UV and visible light per ICH Q1B guidelines.

- **Climatic Zone Testing:**

  - ○ Zone III: 30°C ± 2°C / 35% RH ± 5%.
  - ○ Zone IVa: 30°C ± 2°C / 65% RH ± 5%.
  - ○ Zone IVb: 30°C ± 2°C / 75% RH ± 5%.

5. Testing Frequency
Define the time points for sample analysis:

- **Accelerated Studies:** Initial, 1, 2, 3, and 6 months.
- **Long-Term Studies:** Initial, 3, 6, 9, and 12 months, and then annually.
- **Intermediate Studies:** Initial, 3, and 6 months.

6. Parameters to be Evaluated
Identify the attributes to be monitored to assess stability:

1. **Chemical:** Assay, impurity profile, degradation products.
2. **Physical:** Appearance, hardness, particle size, viscosity.
3. **Microbiological:** Sterility or microbial limits.
4. **Dissolution:** Release profile for oral dosage forms.
5. **Packaging Integrity:** Moisture ingress, oxygen permeability.
6. **pH:** For solutions and suspensions.

7. Analytical Methods

Detail the validated analytical techniques to be used:

- High-Performance Liquid Chromatography (HPLC) for assay and impurities.
- Gas Chromatography (GC) for residual solvents.
- Fourier Transform Infrared Spectroscopy (FTIR) for functional group identification.
- Dissolution apparatus for release testing.

8. Sample Selection and Storage

Specify:

- **Batch Size:** Use representative production-scale or pilot-scale batches.
- **Packaging:** Store samples in the intended final packaging materials (e.g., blister packs, bottles).
- **Storage Conditions:** Use controlled chambers monitored for temperature and humidity.

9. Acceptance Criteria

Establish criteria for each parameter based on regulatory guidelines:

- Assay: Typically 90-110% of the label claim.
- Impurities: Not exceeding specified thresholds.
- Dissolution: Matching reference product release profiles.

10. Documentation and Reporting

Provide detailed records of:

1. Study protocol approval.
2. Raw data for each testing point.

3. Statistical analysis of stability trends.
4. Final report summarizing findings and conclusions.

11. Responsibilities

Define the roles and responsibilities of the teams involved:

- **Quality Assurance (QA):** Approving protocols and reports.
- **R&D Team:** Designing the study and analyzing samples.
- **Production Team:** Providing representative batches.

12. Corrective Actions

Include procedures to address unexpected results:

- Investigating deviations in stability data.
- Implementing changes in formulation, packaging, or storage conditions.

Example Protocol Implementation

For a generic tablet containing amlodipine:

- **Storage Conditions:**

  - Long-term: 25°C / 60% RH for 24 months.
  - Accelerated: 40°C / 75% RH for 6 months.
  - Intermediate: 30°C / 65% RH for 6 months.

- **Parameters Monitored:** Assay, impurities, dissolution, and physical properties.
- **Analytical Method:** HPLC for assay and impurity quantification, dissolution apparatus for release testing.
- **Testing Frequency:** Samples analyzed at 0, 3, 6, 9, and 12 months for long-term studies, and at 0, 1, 2, 3, and 6 months for accelerated studies.

9.3 Accelerated Stability Studies

Accelerated stability studies are a vital component of the drug development process, providing critical information about how a drug product behaves under extreme environmental conditions. These studies are designed to predict the long-term stability of a product in a significantly shorter period by exposing it to elevated temperatures and humidity levels.

Accelerated stability studies help in determining the product's shelf life, storage conditions, and degradation pathways, ensuring the drug's quality, safety, and efficacy.

Purpose of Accelerated Stability Testing

1. **Shelf Life Prediction:**
   Accelerated studies estimate the product's stability over its intended shelf life by extrapolating data collected under stress conditions.
2. **Degradation Pathway Identification:**
   These studies help identify chemical, physical, and microbiological degradation pathways, providing insights into potential stability issues.
3. **Support for Regulatory Submissions:**
   Data from accelerated studies are a mandatory part of regulatory filings, including New Drug Applications (NDAs) and Abbreviated New Drug Applications (ANDAs).
4. **Optimal Packaging and Storage Conditions:**
   Results guide the selection of suitable packaging materials and recommend storage conditions to ensure product stability.
5. **Early Risk Assessment:**
   Accelerated testing detects stability problems early in the development process, allowing timely formulation or packaging modifications.

Key Principles of Accelerated Stability Testing

1. **Arrhenius Equation:**
   Accelerated stability testing is based on the Arrhenius equation, which states that the rate of chemical reactions increases with temperature. By testing at elevated temperatures, the product's degradation rate can be accelerated, allowing prediction of its behavior under normal storage conditions.
2. **Extrapolation:**
   Data from accelerated studies are extrapolated to estimate the product's performance over its shelf life under normal storage conditions.

Procedures for Accelerated Stability Testing

1. **Study Design:**

- Select representative batches: Use production-scale or pilot-scale batches for testing.
- Package samples in the final intended packaging (e.g., blister packs, bottles) to simulate real-world conditions.

2. **Storage Conditions:**

- Store samples at elevated conditions: **40°C ± 2°C and 75% RH ± 5%** (as per ICH Q1A guidelines).
- For regions with extreme climates (e.g., Zone IVb), storage conditions may include **30°C ± 2°C and 75% RH ± 5%.**

3. **Testing Frequency:**

- Analyze samples at predetermined intervals: 0, 1, 2, 3, and 6 months.
- Extend testing if required to confirm trends or address anomalies.

4. **Parameters Monitored:**

- **Chemical Attributes:** Assay, impurity profile, and degradation products.
- **Physical Attributes:** Appearance, hardness, dissolution, and moisture content.
- **Microbiological Attributes:** Sterility or microbial limits (if applicable).
- **Packaging Integrity:** Assessment of moisture ingress and material compatibility.

5. **Analytical Techniques:**

- Use validated methods such as High-Performance Liquid Chromatography (HPLC) for assay and impurities.
- Fourier Transform Infrared Spectroscopy (FTIR) for functional group analysis.
- Dissolution testing for release characteristics.

6. **Data Analysis and Extrapolation:**

- Analyze the rate of degradation under accelerated conditions.
- Use the Arrhenius equation or linear regression to predict the product's stability at normal storage conditions.
- Example: If a product loses 5% of its potency in 6 months at 40°C, its estimated shelf life at 25°C might be extrapolated to 2 years.

Challenges in Accelerated Stability Testing

1. **Non-linear Degradation:**
Some products may not follow the Arrhenius relationship, making extrapolation challenging.
2. **Physical Changes Not Reflective of Real-Time Stability:**
Extreme conditions may cause physical changes, such as tablet capping or discoloration, that are unlikely under normal storage conditions.
3. **Complex Formulations:**
Products with complex formulations, such as emulsions or controlled-release systems, may behave differently under accelerated conditions.

Regulatory Guidelines

1. **ICH Q1A (R2): Stability Testing of New Drug Substances and Products**

   - Provides recommendations for conducting accelerated stability studies for global regulatory compliance.

2. **FDA Guidance:**

   - Emphasizes the importance of accelerated stability testing for determining shelf life and ensuring product quality.

3. **ICH Q1E: Evaluation of Stability Data:**

   - Outlines statistical methods for extrapolating accelerated data to predict long-term stability.

Example Application
For a generic antihypertensive tablet:

- **Storage Conditions:** 40°C ± 2°C and 75% RH ± 5%.
- **Testing Intervals:** 0, 1, 2, 3, and 6 months.
- **Parameters Monitored:**

  - Assay: Must remain within 90-110% of the labeled claim.
  - Impurities: Must not exceed regulatory thresholds (e.g., 0.5%).
  - Dissolution: Release profile must match the reference listed drug.

Results showed a minor impurity increase at 6 months under accelerated conditions, prompting further real-time testing to confirm long-term stability.

9.4 Determination of Expiration Dates

Determining the expiration date of a pharmaceutical product is a critical process in drug development, ensuring that the product remains safe, effective, and of high quality throughout its intended shelf life. The expiration date is established based on stability data derived from rigorous studies under various environmental conditions. Regulatory guidelines, such as those from the ICH and FDA, provide clear criteria for determining the shelf life, which must be supported by scientific evidence.

Criteria for Determining Shelf Life

1. **Stability Data**

   - Stability studies conducted under long-term, accelerated, and sometimes intermediate conditions provide the foundational data.
   - Parameters monitored include assay, impurity levels, dissolution profile, physical appearance, and microbiological attributes.
   - Data trends, such as potency loss or impurity increase, are evaluated to define the product's usable duration.

2. **Critical Quality Attributes (CQAs)**

   - Shelf life is determined by the time the product retains all critical quality attributes within specified limits, including:

     - Potency (e.g., assay within 90-110% of the label claim).
     - Impurity thresholds (e.g., below regulatory limits like 0.5% for unspecified impurities).

- Dissolution profile (e.g., consistent release comparable to the reference product).

3. Degradation Kinetics

- The degradation rate is calculated based on the Arrhenius equation, which correlates reaction rate with temperature.
- This helps predict the product's stability under normal storage conditions.

4. Extrapolation of Accelerated Data

- Stability data obtained from accelerated studies (e.g., 40°C/75% RH for 6 months) are extrapolated to estimate the product's long-term behavior.
- The ICH Q1E guideline outlines statistical methods, such as linear regression, for shelf-life prediction.
- Example: If an assay shows a 1% degradation under accelerated conditions, the estimated shelf life under long-term conditions might be two years.

5. Real-Time Stability Data

- Real-time studies (e.g., 25°C/60% RH for 12 months or more) provide definitive evidence of stability.
- Regulatory agencies often require real-time data to confirm the extrapolated shelf life.

6. Packaging Considerations

- Shelf life is influenced by the container-closure system's ability to protect the product from environmental factors such as moisture, oxygen, and light.
- Example: Tablets in blister packs may have a longer shelf life than those in bulk containers due to better protection against humidity.

7. Environmental Conditions

- Storage conditions for shelf-life determination are based on the climatic zones where the product will be marketed:

  - Zone I and II: 25°C ± 2°C / 60% RH ± 5%.
  - Zone III: 30°C ± 2°C / 35% RH ± 5%.
  - Zone IVa: 30°C ± 2°C / 65% RH ± 5%.
  - Zone IVb: 30°C ± 2°C / 75% RH ± 5%.

8. **Microbiological Stability**

   - For products such as sterile injectables or multi-dose formulations, the ability to maintain sterility or comply with microbial limits is a key determinant of shelf life.

9. **Physical Stability**

   - Changes in physical attributes like color, texture, hardness (for tablets), or viscosity (for liquids) can affect the shelf life.
   - Example: Discoloration in light-sensitive products like ascorbic acid can reduce the product's shelf life.

Regulatory Guidelines

1. **ICH Q1A (R2): Stability Testing of New Drug Substances and Products**

   - Provides criteria for conducting stability studies and determining expiration dates.

2. **ICH Q1E: Evaluation of Stability Data**

   - Details statistical methods for analyzing stability data and extrapolating shelf life.

3. **FDA Guidance on Stability Testing**

   - Emphasizes using real-time and accelerated data to establish scientifically justified expiration dates.

4. **WHO Stability Testing Guidelines**

   - Focuses on requirements for shelf-life determination in different climatic zones.

Statistical Analysis for Shelf Life

1. **Regression Analysis:**

   - Stability data are plotted against time, and regression lines are used to estimate the point at which a critical quality attribute deviates from its acceptable limit.

2. **Confidence Intervals:**

   - Confidence intervals (e.g., 95%) are applied to ensure the shelf-life estimate is statistically robust.

3. **Acceptance Criteria:**

   - Assay: Typically 90-110% of the labeled claim.
   - Impurities: Below specified regulatory thresholds.
   - Dissolution: Matching the reference product profile.

Example Application
For a generic antihypertensive tablet:

- **Long-Term Testing:** Conducted at 25°C/60% RH for 24 months.
- **Accelerated Testing:** Conducted at 40°C/75% RH for 6 months.
- **Results:**

  - Assay remains within 95-105% of the labeled claim.
  - Impurities increase by less than 0.2% under accelerated conditions.
  - Dissolution profile remains consistent.

Based on these results, the product is assigned a shelf life of 24 months with storage conditions of **25°C/60% RH**.

CHAPTER TEN

Packaging Development for Generic Drugs

10.1 Importance of Packaging in Drug Stability

Packaging is a critical component of drug development, serving as a barrier to protect pharmaceutical products from environmental factors that could compromise their stability, safety, and efficacy. For generic drugs, packaging plays a key role in maintaining product integrity, ensuring compliance with regulatory standards, and enhancing patient convenience and adherence. Properly designed packaging systems prevent degradation, contamination, and physical damage, extending the shelf life and preserving the quality of the drug product.

Role of Packaging in Product Integrity

1. **Protection Against Environmental Factors**

   - **Moisture Protection:**
     Packaging materials such as aluminum blisters and high-density polyethylene (HDPE) bottles are used to prevent moisture ingress, which can lead to hydrolysis or physical changes like clumping in tablets.
   - **Light Protection:**
     For light-sensitive drugs, packaging materials like amber glass bottles or opaque blister packs block harmful UV and visible light to prevent photodegradation.
   - **Oxygen Barrier:**
     Laminated films and aluminum foils provide oxygen impermeability, protecting drugs prone to oxidative degradation.

2. Maintenance of Physical Integrity

- Packaging ensures the drug's physical properties remain intact, protecting against crushing, abrasion, and breakage during transportation and storage.
- For instance, blister packs provide individual compartments for tablets or capsules, reducing the risk of cross-contamination or damage.

3. Chemical Compatibility

- Packaging materials must not interact chemically with the drug product.
- For example, polyvinyl chloride (PVC) may not be suitable for highly reactive APIs, as it could release plasticizers or other chemicals.

4. Prevention of Microbial Contamination

- For sterile and liquid formulations, hermetically sealed containers such as ampoules or multi-dose vials with preservatives ensure microbial safety.

5. Regulation of Shelf Life

- Packaging acts as a primary determinant of shelf life by creating a controlled microenvironment that mitigates external risks.
- Example: Using desiccants in HDPE bottles for moisture-sensitive drugs extends shelf life by reducing humidity.

6. Facilitating Patient Compliance

- Packaging that is easy to open, resealable, and provides clear dosage instructions promotes proper usage and adherence.
- Example: Calendar blister packs allow patients to track doses more effectively.

Types of Packaging Systems

1. **Primary Packaging**

   - Directly in contact with the drug product.
   - Examples:

     - Blister packs: Common for solid oral dosage forms.
     - Bottles: Used for tablets, capsules, and liquids.
     - Tubes: Suitable for topical creams and ointments.

2. **Secondary Packaging**

   - Provides additional protection and supports branding and patient information.
   - Examples:

     - Outer cartons: Protect against physical damage.
     - Leaflets: Contain usage instructions and regulatory information.

3. **Tertiary Packaging**

   - Used for bulk handling and transportation.
   - Examples:

     - Shipping cartons: Ensure safe delivery of bulk quantities.

Considerations in Packaging Development

1. **Drug Properties**

   - Stability of the API and excipients under various conditions determines the choice of packaging material.
   - Example: A hygroscopic API like losartan requires moisture-proof packaging such as aluminum blisters.

2. **Regulatory Requirements**

   - Packaging must comply with regulatory guidelines like those from the FDA, EMA, or ICH.

- Requirements include material safety, sterility for injectables, and child-resistant closures.

3. **Environmental Impact**

   - Sustainable packaging materials such as recyclable plastics and biodegradable films are increasingly preferred to reduce environmental impact.

4. **Cost Effectiveness**

   - Packaging development must balance protective functionality with economic feasibility to ensure affordability for generic drugs.

5. **Tamper-Evidence**

   - Tamper-evident seals and closures are mandatory for ensuring product safety and consumer trust.

Testing and Validation of Packaging

1. **Moisture Permeability Testing**

   - Determines the rate of moisture ingress through the packaging material.

2. **Light Transmission Testing**

   - Evaluates the packaging's ability to block UV and visible light.

3. **Seal Integrity Testing**

   - Ensures airtight seals to prevent contamination and preserve product stability.

4. **Compatibility Testing**

- Assesses interactions between the packaging material and the drug product to ensure no leachables or extractables compromise the product.

5. **Drop and Shock Testing**

- Simulates transportation conditions to ensure the packaging can withstand physical stress.

Example Application
For a generic antihypertensive tablet like amlodipine:

- **Primary Packaging**: Aluminum-aluminum blister packs protect against both moisture and light.
- **Secondary Packaging**: Outer cartons provide physical protection and include regulatory labeling.
- **Tertiary Packaging**: Shipping cartons with cushioning protect bulk packs during transportation.
- Stability studies confirm that the chosen packaging maintains drug potency and appearance over the designated shelf life.

10.2 Selection of Packaging Materials
The selection of packaging materials for pharmaceutical products is a crucial aspect of drug development. The primary purpose of packaging is to protect the drug product from environmental factors, physical damage, and contamination, while also ensuring patient safety, convenience, and compliance. Packaging materials are chosen based on the properties of the drug, regulatory requirements, and cost considerations. Different types of packaging are used depending on the dosage form, intended market, and specific protection needs.
Types of Packaging Materials

1. **Blister Packs**

- **Description:**
Blister packs consist of individual compartments for tablets or capsules, typically made of thermoformed plastic (e.g., PVC, PVDC) with a lidding material such as aluminum foil.

- **Applications:**
  Commonly used for solid oral dosage forms like tablets and capsules.
- **Advantages:**

  - Provides excellent protection against moisture and light when aluminum-based.
  - Individual compartments prevent cross-contamination and physical damage.
  - Supports patient compliance with labeled dosing instructions or calendar-based packs.

- **Limitations:**

  - PVC may not offer sufficient moisture protection for highly hygroscopic drugs unless layered with PVDC.

2. **Bottles**

- **Description:**
  Plastic or glass bottles are commonly used for tablets, capsules, and liquid formulations.
- **Plastic Bottles:**

  - Material: High-density polyethylene (HDPE), polypropylene (PP), or polyethylene terephthalate (PET).
  - Applications: Suitable for tablets and capsules.
  - Features: Lightweight, shatterproof, and moisture-resistant.

- **Glass Bottles:**

  - Material: Amber or clear glass.
  - Applications: Common for liquid formulations or light-sensitive APIs.
  - Features: Chemically inert and impermeable to oxygen.

- **Advantages:**

  - Accommodates larger quantities compared to blister packs.

- Can include child-resistant closures for safety.

- **Limitations:**

    - Glass bottles are heavier and more prone to breakage.
    - Plastic bottles may allow minimal moisture permeation.

3. **Ampoules and Vials**

- **Description:**
  Ampoules are single-use sealed glass containers, while vials are multi-dose containers made of glass or plastic.
- **Applications:**
  Common for injectables, vaccines, and ophthalmic preparations.
- **Advantages:**

    - Glass ampoules are inert and provide excellent protection for sterile products.
    - Vials with rubber stoppers allow repeated access for multi-dose applications.

- **Limitations:**

    - Ampoules require careful handling to avoid breakage.

4. **Sachets and Pouches**

- **Description:**
  Flexible packaging materials, often laminated with layers of plastic and aluminum, used for powders, granules, or liquids.
- **Applications:**
  Suitable for single-dose sachets or bulk pouches.
- **Advantages:**

    - Cost-effective and lightweight.
    - Provides good barrier properties for moisture-sensitive products.

- **Limitations:**

- Less robust compared to rigid packaging options.

5. Tubes

- **Description:**
  Metal (aluminum) or plastic (laminated) tubes used for topical formulations like creams, gels, and ointments.
- **Applications:**
  Dermatological or cosmetic preparations.
- **Advantages:**

  - Protects product integrity by preventing contamination and evaporation.
  - Allows controlled dispensing.

- **Limitations:**

  - Aluminum tubes can deform and are sensitive to physical stress.

6. Syringes and Cartridge Systems

- **Description:**
  Pre-filled syringes or cartridges made of plastic or glass, used for injectable formulations.
- **Applications:**
  Vaccines, insulin, and other injectable drugs.
- **Advantages:**

  - Facilitates easy and accurate dosing.
  - Reduces the risk of contamination.

- **Limitations:**

  - Higher cost compared to traditional vials.

7. Strip Packs

- ◦ **Description:**
  Individual units sealed between aluminum or plastic layers.
- ◦ **Applications:**
  Ideal for moisture-sensitive tablets or powders.
- ◦ **Advantages:**

  - Excellent moisture and oxygen barrier properties.
  - Easy to transport and store.

- ◦ **Limitations:**

  - Less visually appealing than blister packs.

8. **Other Specialized Packaging**

   - ◦ **Desiccant Packs:**

     - Used within bottles or blister packs to absorb moisture and protect hygroscopic drugs.

   - ◦ **Cold Chain Packaging:**

     - Insulated containers designed for temperature-sensitive biologics or vaccines.

   - ◦ **Modified Atmosphere Packaging (MAP):**

     - Uses inert gases to prevent oxidative degradation in sensitive APIs.

Factors Influencing Material Selection

1. **Drug Properties:**

   - ◦ Hygroscopic drugs require moisture-proof materials like aluminum or PVDC.
   - ◦ Light-sensitive APIs need opaque packaging such as amber glass or aluminum foil.

2. **Regulatory Requirements:**

   - Packaging must meet guidelines for material safety, child-resistance, and tamper evidence set by regulatory authorities like the FDA, EMA, and WHO.

3. **Environmental Impact:**

   - Increasing preference for recyclable or biodegradable packaging materials to reduce environmental impact.

4. **Cost and Feasibility:**

   - Packaging development must balance functionality with affordability, especially for generic products targeting competitive markets.

5. **Patient Convenience and Compliance:**

   - User-friendly designs, such as easy-to-open closures and labeled doses, improve adherence.

Example Applications

For a generic antihypertensive tablet like losartan:

- **Blister Packs:** PVDC-coated aluminum for moisture protection and patient convenience.
- **Bottles:** HDPE bottles with desiccants for bulk packaging in pharmacies.
- **Strip Packs:** Used in resource-limited settings for cost efficiency and protection.

For a sterile injectable like insulin:

- **Primary Packaging:** Glass vials with rubber stoppers or pre-filled syringes for ease of administration.
- **Secondary Packaging:** Insulated containers for cold chain storage.

10.3 Testing of Packaging Systems

Testing of packaging systems is an essential part of pharmaceutical product development, ensuring that the chosen packaging adequately protects the drug product from environmental and physical factors while remaining compatible with the drug's formulation. Robust testing validates the packaging's performance in maintaining product stability, integrity, and safety throughout its shelf life. Key aspects include barrier properties and compatibility testing, which assess the material's ability to shield the product from moisture, light, oxygen, and potential chemical interactions.

Barrier Properties Testing

Barrier properties refer to the packaging material's ability to prevent external factors such as moisture, oxygen, and light from interacting with the drug product. The following tests are commonly performed:

1. **Moisture Barrier Testing**

   - **Purpose:** To evaluate the packaging's resistance to moisture ingress, critical for hygroscopic drugs prone to hydrolysis.
   - **Test Methods:**

     - **Gravimetric Method:** Measures weight change in a controlled humidity chamber to determine moisture absorption.
     - **Water Vapor Transmission Rate (WVTR):** Assesses the rate at which moisture passes through the material.
     - **Example:** Aluminum foils exhibit near-zero WVTR, making them ideal for moisture-sensitive drugs.

2. **Oxygen Barrier Testing**

   - **Purpose:** To measure the material's ability to prevent oxygen penetration, crucial for APIs prone to oxidative degradation.
   - **Test Methods:**

     - **Oxygen Transmission Rate (OTR):** Quantifies the amount of oxygen passing through the packaging over time.
     - **Permeation Tests:** Evaluate oxygen ingress under controlled conditions.

- ◦ **Example:** Laminated aluminum films provide excellent oxygen barrier properties.

3. **Light Transmission Testing**

   - ◦ **Purpose:** To assess the material's ability to block harmful UV and visible light that may degrade light-sensitive APIs.
   - ◦ **Test Methods:**

     - ▪ UV-visible spectrophotometry is used to measure light transmittance through the packaging material.

   - ◦ **Example:** Amber glass and opaque blister packs are used for light-sensitive drugs like ascorbic acid.

4. **Seal Integrity Testing**

   - ◦ **Purpose:** To ensure the packaging's seals are airtight and prevent ingress of contaminants or gases.
   - ◦ **Test Methods:**

     - ▪ **Vacuum Leak Test:** Detects leaks by applying a vacuum and observing for pressure changes.
     - ▪ **Dye Penetration Test:** Uses a colored dye to detect potential leaks.

Compatibility Testing

Compatibility testing evaluates the interaction between the drug product and the packaging material to ensure that no harmful leachables, extractables, or chemical reactions occur during storage.

1. **Extractables and Leachables Testing**

   - ◦ **Purpose:** To identify substances that could migrate from the packaging material into the drug product.
   - ◦ **Extractables Testing:**

     - ▪ Simulates extreme conditions (e.g., high temperature, aggressive solvents) to identify potential extractable compounds.

- ○ **Leachables Testing:**

  - ▪ Simulates real-world storage conditions to assess what substances may leach into the product over time.

- ○ **Example:** Plastic packaging materials like PVC or HDPE are tested to ensure no harmful chemicals migrate into the drug.

2. **Chemical Compatibility**

   - ○ **Purpose:** To ensure that the packaging material does not react chemically with the drug product or its excipients.
   - ○ **Test Methods:**

     - ▪ Stability studies where the drug is stored in the intended packaging material, and chemical analyses are conducted to detect degradation or interaction.

   - ○ **Example:** Certain formulations containing alcohol may dissolve plasticizers from PVC, requiring alternative materials like PET.

3. **Physical Compatibility**

   - ○ **Purpose:** To confirm that physical interactions, such as adsorption or absorption, do not alter the drug product's quality.
   - ○ **Test Methods:**

     - ▪ Testing for drug adsorption onto packaging surfaces or loss of liquid formulations due to material absorption.

   - ○ **Example:** Protein-based biologics may adsorb to glass vials, necessitating the use of siliconized glass.

4. **Functional Compatibility**

   - ○ **Purpose:** To ensure that packaging systems perform their intended function, such as resealing, dosing accuracy, or protection during use.
   - ○ **Test Methods:**

- Functional tests for closures, caps, or child-resistant mechanisms.

- **Example:** Multi-dose vials with rubber stoppers are tested for reseal integrity.

Additional Tests for Packaging Systems

1. **Drop and Shock Testing**

   - Simulates shipping and handling conditions to assess packaging durability against impact and vibration.
   - Example: Cartons are subjected to repeated drops to ensure the inner drug product remains undamaged.

2. **Thermal Stress Testing**

   - Evaluates packaging performance under extreme temperatures to ensure stability during transport and storage.
   - Example: Cold chain packaging for vaccines is tested under -20°C to 40°C conditions.

3. **Compression Testing**

   - Assesses the packaging's ability to withstand weight during stacking or bulk storage.
   - Example: Plastic bottles are compressed to ensure they don't deform under normal warehouse conditions.

4. **Microbial Barrier Testing**

   - Verifies that the packaging prevents microbial ingress for sterile products.
   - Example: Sterility testing is performed on vials used for injectables.

Regulatory Guidelines

1. **ICH Guidelines**

- ◦ ICH Q1A (R2): Addresses packaging requirements in stability studies.
- ◦ ICH Q3C: Guidance on extractables and leachables in pharmaceutical packaging.

2. **USP and FDA Requirements**

- ◦ USP <661>: Guidelines for plastic packaging.
- ◦ USP <671>: Requirements for performance tests on packaging systems.

3. **ISO Standards**

- ◦ ISO 11607: Guidelines for packaging systems used in sterile medical products.
- ◦ ISO 15189: Specifies environmental testing for packaging systems.

Example Application
For a generic tablet:

- **Barrier Properties Testing:** Aluminum-PVC blister packs are tested for WVTR, OTR, and UV light transmission to ensure protection against moisture, oxygen, and light.
- **Compatibility Testing:** Stability studies confirm that the API remains chemically stable in the blister packs without interaction with the PVC or aluminum.

For an injectable:

- **Barrier Properties Testing:** Glass vials with rubber stoppers undergo microbial barrier testing and oxygen permeation tests.

Compatibility Testing: Extractables testing confirms that no harmful chemicals leach from the stopper into the drug solution

CHAPTER ELEVEN

Scale-Up and Technology Transfer

11.1 Scaling from Lab to Pilot and Production Batches

Scaling up from laboratory-scale formulations to pilot and production-scale batches is a crucial phase in pharmaceutical manufacturing. It ensures that the processes developed in the lab can be efficiently reproduced on a larger scale without compromising the quality, safety, and efficacy of the drug product. This transition involves meticulous planning, process optimization, and validation to address potential challenges and meet regulatory standards.

Key Steps in Scaling Up

1. **Process Understanding and Optimization**

   - Before scaling up, the laboratory-scale process must be thoroughly studied and optimized.
   - Critical Process Parameters (CPPs) and Critical Quality Attributes (CQAs) are identified to ensure consistent product quality.
   - Example: Mixing time, blending uniformity, and granulation parameters for tablets are optimized.

2. **Selection of Equipment**

   - Equipment used for production-scale batches must mimic lab-scale processes to maintain product equivalence.
   - Scale-independent parameters, such as mixing intensity, drying time, and granule size, are considered.

- ◦ Example: Fluidized bed dryers are validated for both lab and production scales to ensure consistency.

3. Pilot Batches

- ◦ Pilot-scale batches (typically 10-100 kg) act as an intermediary step between lab and full-scale production.
- ◦ These batches provide data on process feasibility, equipment suitability, and scalability.
- ◦ Critical observations during pilot batches include yield, uniformity, and process reproducibility.

4. Production-Scale Batches

- ◦ Full-scale batches (greater than 100 kg) are manufactured after successful pilot trials.
- ◦ Process validation is conducted to demonstrate that the production process consistently produces batches meeting predetermined specifications.
- ◦ Example: Uniform tablet hardness and dissolution profiles are verified for production-scale batches.

5. Validation and Documentation

- ◦ Comprehensive validation of the scaled-up process is required to ensure reproducibility and compliance with regulatory standards.
- ◦ Process Validation includes:

  - **Installation Qualification (IQ):** Ensures equipment installation meets design specifications.
  - **Operational Qualification (OQ):** Verifies equipment performance under specified conditions.
  - **Performance Qualification (PQ):** Confirms the process yields consistent results at scale.

Challenges in Scaling Up

1. Process Variability

- Small changes in parameters like temperature, mixing speed, or feed rate can lead to significant differences in product quality.
- Example: Over-granulation during large-scale wet granulation may alter dissolution profiles.

2. **Equipment Differences**

- Scale-up often involves switching from lab-scale to larger, industrial-scale equipment, which may not directly correlate.
- Adjustments in parameters like shear force, drying rates, or compression force are needed.

3. **Material Handling**

- Managing large volumes of raw materials introduces challenges in uniformity, segregation, and flow properties.
- Example: Flowability issues in large-scale powder handling can lead to non-uniform blending.

4. **Environmental Factors**

- Large-scale production may expose the product to additional environmental conditions such as prolonged exposure to air or humidity, potentially affecting stability.

5. **Cost and Time Constraints**

- Scaling up requires significant resources for equipment, testing, and validation, increasing overall costs and timelines.

Best Practices for Successful Scale-Up

1. **Quality by Design (QbD) Approach**

- Incorporating QbD principles ensures a thorough understanding of process variability and allows for better control strategies.
- Example: Design of Experiments (DoE) is used to optimize blending time and compression force.

2. **Simulation and Modeling**

   - Use computational tools to simulate large-scale processes based on lab-scale data, reducing trial-and-error approaches.
   - Example: Predicting mixing uniformity or drying kinetics using process simulation software.

3. **Real-Time Monitoring**

   - Implement Process Analytical Technology (PAT) tools for in-line monitoring of critical quality attributes.
   - Example: Near-infrared spectroscopy (NIR) is used to monitor blend uniformity in real time.

4. **Collaboration and Communication**

   - Effective coordination between R&D, manufacturing, and quality assurance teams ensures smooth scale-up and problem resolution.

5. **Regulatory Compliance**

   - Adhere to cGMP guidelines and document all scale-up activities to meet regulatory requirements.
   - Ensure traceability and accountability in all processes.

Example Application

For a generic extended-release tablet:

1. **Lab Scale:** Formulation developed with 100-gram batches using a small-scale fluid bed granulator.
2. **Pilot Scale:** Batch size increased to 10 kg with adjustments to drying time and granulator airflow. Yield and tablet uniformity are validated.
3. **Production Scale:** Full-scale batches of 500 kg manufactured using industrial-scale granulators and tablet presses. Process parameters like compression force and coating time are optimized and validated.
4. **Validation:** Three consecutive production batches are validated to confirm consistent dissolution profiles and API content.

Key Challenges in the Scale-Up Process

Scaling up pharmaceutical manufacturing from lab-scale to pilot-scale and then to full-scale production involves several complexities. Addressing these challenges is critical to maintaining the quality, safety, and efficacy of the drug product while ensuring cost-effectiveness and compliance with regulatory requirements. Below are the key challenges encountered during the scale-up process:

1. Process Variability

- Scaling up involves larger equipment and increased material volumes, leading to variations in critical parameters such as mixing, heating, and drying.
- Example: Differences in shear forces in small vs. large mixers can affect granule size, impacting dissolution and bioavailability.

2. Equipment and Technology Differences

- Lab-scale equipment may not directly correlate with industrial-scale machinery, requiring adjustments to process parameters.
- Example: A fluidized bed dryer may have different air distribution and drying rates at scale, requiring re-optimization.

3. Material Handling and Flow Properties

- Handling large quantities of raw materials may introduce challenges like segregation, bridging, and flow inconsistencies.
- Example: Powder segregation during large-scale mixing can lead to non-uniform blending.

4. Environmental Factors

- Scaling up may expose materials to additional environmental factors such as humidity, temperature, and airflow, which can impact stability.
- Example: Hygroscopic APIs may absorb moisture during prolonged exposure in large-scale production.

5. Reproducibility of Lab Processes

- Processes optimized for small-scale operations may not behave identically when scaled up.
- Example: Over-granulation during wet granulation in large-scale production can alter tablet hardness and dissolution profiles.

6. Cost and Resource Requirements

- Scaling up requires significant investment in equipment, process validation, and personnel training, increasing overall project costs.

7. Quality and Regulatory Compliance

- Ensuring that scale-up activities meet stringent cGMP and regulatory requirements is challenging, especially with complex formulations.

8. Time Constraints

- Scaling up often needs to meet tight deadlines to ensure timely market entry, leaving limited time for troubleshooting and optimization.

11.2 Process Validation During Scale-Up

Process validation is a critical component of the scale-up process, ensuring that the manufacturing process consistently produces drug products meeting predetermined quality standards. This step is essential for compliance with regulatory requirements and achieving reproducible, high-quality production at commercial scales.

Purpose of Process Validation

- To demonstrate that the scaled-up manufacturing process operates within established parameters and produces consistent, high-quality products.
- To identify and control critical process parameters (CPPs) and critical quality attributes (CQAs).

Key Phases of Process Validation

1. **Stage 1: Process Design**

- Develop a thorough understanding of the manufacturing process during lab-scale and pilot-scale studies.
- Identify CPPs that impact CQAs, such as blending time, drying temperature, and compression force.
- Example: A wet granulation process may require optimization of granulation fluid addition rate and mixer speed.

2. Stage 2: Process Qualification

- Validate the scaled-up process using full-scale equipment and commercial-scale batches.
- Conduct Installation Qualification (IQ), Operational Qualification (OQ), and Performance Qualification (PQ).

  - **IQ:** Ensures equipment is installed according to specifications.
  - **OQ:** Verifies that equipment performs as intended under specified conditions.
  - **PQ:** Confirms that the process consistently produces products meeting quality standards.

3. Stage 3: Continued Process Verification

- Implement real-time monitoring during routine manufacturing to ensure ongoing control and consistency.
- Example: Use Process Analytical Technology (PAT) tools like near-infrared spectroscopy (NIR) to monitor blend uniformity.

Steps to Ensure Consistency During Manufacturing

1. Define Process Parameters

- Establish acceptable operating ranges for CPPs, such as mixing time, granulation temperature, and coating thickness.
- Use Design of Experiments (DoE) to optimize and understand parameter interactions.

2. Conduct Trial Runs

- ◦ Perform multiple pilot-scale and full-scale runs to identify potential bottlenecks and variability.
- ◦ Example: Adjust fluidized bed drying times to achieve uniform moisture content.

3. **Validation of Equipment**

- ◦ Ensure that all equipment used in production is calibrated and validated to function correctly at the required scale.
- ◦ Example: Tablet presses must produce tablets with uniform weight, hardness, and thickness.

4. **Sampling and Testing**

- ◦ Collect in-process samples to test CQAs, such as API content, granule size, and dissolution rates.
- ◦ Example: Tablets sampled during compression are tested for uniformity and friability.

5. **Risk Assessment and Mitigation**

- ◦ Identify potential risks during scale-up using tools like Failure Mode and Effects Analysis (FMEA) and implement mitigation strategies.
- ◦ Example: Implement humidity controls for hygroscopic APIs.

6. **Documentation**

- ◦ Maintain detailed records of all validation activities, including batch records, test results, and deviations.
- ◦ Example: A comprehensive validation report includes data on blending uniformity, assay results, and equipment performance.

Regulatory Requirements for Validation

1. **FDA Guidelines**

- ◦ Follow FDA's Process Validation Guidance, which emphasizes a lifecycle approach to validation.

- Submit validation data as part of the New Drug Application (NDA) or Abbreviated New Drug Application (ANDA).

2. **ICH Q8, Q9, Q10 Guidelines**

- ICH Q8: Emphasizes Quality by Design (QbD) principles.
- ICH Q9: Focuses on risk management.
- ICH Q10: Provides a framework for quality systems during validation.

3. **EU Guidelines**

- European Medicines Agency (EMA) requires process validation data for marketing authorization applications.

Example Application

For a generic oral tablet:

- **Pilot Scale:** A 50-kg batch is produced to optimize blending time and granule size.
- **Full-Scale Production:** A 500-kg batch is manufactured with validated mixing and compression processes.
- **Validation:**

  - Blending uniformity is tested using NIR spectroscopy.
  - Finished tablets are tested for assay, dissolution, and physical attributes like hardness and thickness.

- **Outcome:** Validation confirms that the scaled-up process consistently produces high-quality tablets meeting regulatory requirements.

11.3 Technology Transfer from R&D to Manufacturing

Technology transfer is a critical phase in pharmaceutical development, involving the transition of knowledge, processes, and technologies from research and development (R&D) to full-scale manufacturing. This step ensures that the product developed in the lab can be consistently produced at a commercial scale while maintaining quality, efficacy, and safety. Effective technology transfer minimizes risks, streamlines production, and facilitates compliance with regulatory requirements.

Key Elements of Technology Transfer

1. **Knowledge Transfer**

   - Sharing detailed information about the product's formulation, process parameters, equipment requirements, and analytical methods from R&D to manufacturing teams.

2. **Process Scale-Up**

   - Adapting small-scale lab processes to production-scale equipment while maintaining consistency and quality.

3. **Regulatory Compliance**

   - Ensuring that the technology transfer process adheres to cGMP guidelines and meets regulatory standards set by agencies such as the FDA, EMA, and WHO.

4. **Documentation**

   - Comprehensive documentation is essential for a smooth transfer, providing clear instructions and records for all stages of production.

Documentation Requirements for Technology Transfer

Documentation serves as the backbone of the technology transfer process, ensuring traceability, reproducibility, and regulatory compliance. Key documents include:

1. **Technology Transfer Plan (TTP)**

   - Outlines the scope, objectives, timelines, and responsibilities for the transfer process.
   - Includes key milestones such as validation and production timelines.

2. **Master Formula Record (MFR)**

- Provides detailed instructions for manufacturing the product, including raw material specifications, process steps, and in-process controls.

3. **Process Development Report (PDR)**

   - Summarizes all process development activities, including optimization studies, process parameters, and risk assessments.
   - Example: Describes the granulation method, mixing time, and drying parameters for tablet production.

4. **Analytical Method Transfer Report**

   - Documents the transfer of validated analytical methods from R&D to the quality control (QC) laboratory.
   - Includes test methods for assay, dissolution, impurity profiling, and microbiological testing.

5. **Validation Protocols and Reports**

   - Cover process validation, equipment qualification (IQ/OQ/PQ), and analytical method validation.
   - Example: A validation protocol for tablet compression includes testing for weight uniformity, hardness, and friability.

6. **Training Records**

   - Document training sessions conducted for manufacturing personnel on new processes, equipment, and QC methods.

7. **Deviation and Change Control Records**

   - Document any deviations from standard procedures or changes made during the transfer process.

8. **Standard Operating Procedures (SOPs)**

- Provide step-by-step instructions for all production and testing activities, tailored to the manufacturing environment.

Best Practices for Technology Transfer

1. **Cross-Functional Collaboration**

   - Establish a technology transfer team comprising R&D, manufacturing, quality assurance (QA), quality control (QC), and regulatory affairs personnel.
   - Regular meetings ensure clear communication and address challenges promptly.

2. **Risk Assessment and Mitigation**

   - Identify potential risks, such as equipment differences or material variability, using tools like Failure Mode and Effects Analysis (FMEA).
   - Develop mitigation strategies, such as parameter adjustments or additional training.

3. **Pilot Batches**

   - Produce pilot-scale batches to test the process under production-scale conditions and identify any challenges before full-scale manufacturing.
   - Example: A pilot batch for a controlled-release tablet tests coating uniformity and release profiles.

4. **Process and Analytical Validation**

   - Validate all processes and analytical methods under production conditions to ensure consistency and compliance.
   - Example: Validate the dissolution test method for both R&D and QC environments.

5. **Knowledge Sharing and Training**

- Provide comprehensive training for manufacturing personnel to familiarize them with the new process and equipment.
- Use training aids like videos, manuals, and hands-on demonstrations.

6. Real-Time Monitoring

- Implement Process Analytical Technology (PAT) tools to monitor critical process parameters in real-time, ensuring consistent quality.
- Example: Use near-infrared spectroscopy (NIR) to monitor blend uniformity during production.

7. Regulatory Alignment

- Ensure that all transfer activities are documented and aligned with regulatory requirements.
- Prepare regulatory submission dossiers, such as NDAs or ANDAs, based on validated processes.

8. Post-Transfer Support

- Provide ongoing support to the manufacturing team to resolve any issues that arise during initial production runs.
- Establish feedback mechanisms to continuously improve the process.

Challenges in Technology Transfer

1. Equipment and Facility Differences

- Scaling up from R&D to manufacturing often involves different equipment sizes and configurations, requiring process adjustments.

2. Process Reproducibility

- Ensuring that small-scale processes behave consistently at a larger scale can be challenging.

3. Material Variability

- Variations in raw material properties, such as particle size or flowability, can impact process performance.

4. **Regulatory Compliance**

- Adhering to stringent cGMP and regulatory guidelines requires meticulous planning and documentation.

Example Application
Technology Transfer for an Extended-Release Tablet:

1. **Knowledge Transfer:** Detailed process parameters for granulation, compression, and coating are shared with the manufacturing team.
2. **Pilot Batch:** A 10-kg batch is produced to test process feasibility and identify potential challenges.
3. **Validation:** Equipment is qualified, and the process is validated with three consecutive production-scale batches of 500 kg.
4. **Training:** Manufacturing and QC personnel are trained on the new process and analytical methods.
5. **Post-Transfer Monitoring:** Initial production runs are monitored to ensure consistent quality and address any deviations.

CHAPTER TWELVE

Bioequivalence Studies: Design and Conduct

12.1 Introduction to Bioequivalence Studies

Bioequivalence (BE) studies are critical for demonstrating that a generic drug performs in the same manner as its reference listed drug (RLD) in terms of safety, efficacy, and pharmacokinetic (PK) properties. Regulatory agencies, including the US FDA, EMA, and CDSCO, require these studies as part of the approval process for generic drugs. The primary objective is to ensure that the generic product is therapeutically equivalent to the RLD, providing the same clinical benefit to patients.

Definition and Purpose of Bioequivalence Studies

1. **Definition:**

   Bioequivalence is defined as the absence of a significant difference in the rate and extent of drug absorption when a test product (generic) is compared to a reference product (RLD) under similar experimental conditions.

2. **Purpose:**

   - To establish therapeutic equivalence between a generic product and the RLD.
   - To ensure that the generic drug delivers the same amount of active pharmaceutical ingredient (API) to the systemic circulation as the reference product.
   - To support regulatory submissions for marketing authorization of generic drugs.

Regulatory Basis

1. **FDA Guidance:**
   The FDA requires BE studies for approval of Abbreviated New Drug Applications (ANDAs) to ensure interchangeability between the generic product and the RLD.
2. **ICH Guidelines:**
   ICH E5 outlines the importance of BE studies in ensuring consistency across different populations.
3. **WHO Guidelines:**
   WHO emphasizes BE studies to support global harmonization of generic drug approvals.

When Are Bioequivalence Studies Required?

1. **Generic Drug Approvals:**
   Required for ANDAs to demonstrate equivalence to the RLD.
2. **Post-Approval Changes:**
   Conducted when significant changes are made to the formulation, manufacturing process, or site of production.
3. **New Formulations of Approved Drugs:**
   Required for modified-release formulations or alternative dosage forms.

Key Parameters Evaluated in BE Studies

1. **Pharmacokinetics (PK):**

   - **Cmax (Maximum Plasma Concentration):** Indicates the peak drug concentration in plasma.
   - **Tmax (Time to Reach Cmax):** Measures the rate of absorption.
   - **AUC (Area Under the Curve):** Represents the extent of drug absorption.

2. **Statistical Criteria:**

   - BE is established if the 90% confidence interval (CI) of the ratio of the test product to the reference product for Cmax and AUC falls within the acceptable range of 80-125%.

Advantages of Bioequivalence Studies

1. **Cost-Effectiveness:**

   ◦ Eliminates the need for large-scale clinical trials, reducing the cost of generic drug development.

2. **Regulatory Assurance:**

   ◦ Provides a scientific basis for regulatory approval, ensuring product quality and safety.

3. **Therapeutic Interchangeability:**

   ◦ Confirms that patients can safely switch between the generic product and the RLD without compromising therapeutic outcomes.

Challenges in Conducting BE Studies

1. **High Variability Drugs:**

   ◦ Drugs with high intra-subject variability in PK parameters require special designs and statistical approaches.

2. **Complex Formulations:**

   ◦ Modified-release or combination products present unique challenges in achieving BE.

3. **Special Populations:**

   ◦ Conducting BE studies in populations like pediatrics or geriatrics requires careful ethical and logistical considerations.

Example Application
For a generic extended-release tablet:

- **Objective:** Demonstrate BE with the RLD under fasting and fed conditions.
- **Design:** Randomized, crossover study in healthy volunteers.

- **Outcome:** The test product achieves a 90% CI for Cmax and AUC within 80-125%, confirming BE.

12.2 Study Designs for Bioequivalence

The design of a bioequivalence (BE) study is crucial to accurately assess the pharmacokinetic (PK) equivalence between a test product (generic) and a reference listed drug (RLD). Study designs must align with regulatory requirements, ensuring reliable results while minimizing variability and ethical concerns. The most common designs include parallel, crossover, and replicate designs, each chosen based on the characteristics of the drug, the study population, and specific regulatory guidance.

1. Parallel Design

In a parallel design, two separate groups of subjects are used:

- One group receives the test product.
- The other group receives the reference product.

Characteristics:

- **Population:** Two distinct groups of healthy volunteers or patients.
- **Procedure:** Each subject receives only one treatment (test or reference) during the study period.

Advantages:

1. Simpler to conduct compared to crossover designs.
2. Suitable for drugs with long half-lives, where washout periods would be impractical.
3. Eliminates the risk of carryover effects since each subject receives only one treatment.

Disadvantages:

1. Requires a larger sample size to account for inter-subject variability.
2. Higher costs due to the need for more participants.

Example:

A parallel design is often used for biologics or long-acting formulations such as depot injections.

2. Crossover Design

In a crossover design, each subject receives both the test and reference products in two separate periods, with a washout period in between to eliminate residual effects of the first treatment.

Characteristics:

- **Population:** Single group of subjects serves as their own control.
- **Procedure:** Subjects are randomly assigned to receive the test product in one period and the reference product in the other period.

Advantages:

1. Reduces inter-subject variability by allowing direct comparison within the same individual.
2. Requires a smaller sample size than a parallel design.
3. Widely accepted for BE studies due to high statistical power.

Disadvantages:

1. Risk of carryover effects if the washout period is insufficient.
2. Not suitable for drugs with long half-lives or irreversible pharmacological effects.

Example:

Crossover designs are commonly used for oral solid dosage forms like tablets and capsules, especially for immediate-release formulations.

3. Replicate Design

Replicate designs are an extension of crossover designs, where each subject receives the test and reference products multiple times. These designs are particularly useful for highly variable drugs (HVDs) with significant intra-subject PK variability.

Characteristics:

- **Population:** A single group of subjects receives the same treatment (test or reference) multiple times.

- **Procedure:** Subjects follow sequences such as Test-Reference-Test-Reference (TRTR) or Reference-Test-Reference-Test (RTRT).

Advantages:

1. Allows for precise estimation of intra-subject variability.
2. Suitable for highly variable drugs where traditional designs might fail to meet BE criteria.
3. Enables scaled average bioequivalence (SABE), which adjusts for high variability in PK parameters.

Disadvantages:

1. More complex to design and analyze.
2. Longer study duration due to multiple dosing periods.
3. Requires larger sample sizes compared to simple crossover designs.

Example:

Replicate designs are often used for modified-release formulations or drugs with high variability in PK parameters such as cyclosporine or warfarin.

Factors Influencing Study Design Selection

1. **Drug Properties:**

   - Long half-life drugs are better suited for parallel designs to avoid extended washout periods.
   - Highly variable drugs often require replicate designs to account for intra-subject variability.

2. **Subject Characteristics:**

   - Crossover designs are ideal for studies involving healthy volunteers.
   - Parallel designs may be preferred for patient populations to simplify logistics.

3. **Regulatory Requirements:**

- Regulatory agencies like the FDA and EMA provide specific guidelines for choosing appropriate study designs based on the drug type and intended market.

4. **Cost and Resources:**

- Parallel designs may incur higher costs due to larger sample sizes, while replicate designs may demand more complex data analysis.

Example Applications

1. **Immediate-Release Tablet:**

   - **Design:** Crossover.
   - **Rationale:** Short half-life drug with minimal carryover risk and low variability.

2. **Long-Acting Injectable:**

   - **Design:** Parallel.
   - **Rationale:** Long half-life requiring impractically lengthy washout periods in a crossover study.

3. **Highly Variable Drug:**

   - **Design:** Replicate.
   - **Rationale:** Accounts for intra-subject variability and allows SABE analysis.

Key Pharmacokinetic Parameters

1. **AUC (Area Under the Curve)**

   - **Definition:** Represents the total exposure of the drug in the bloodstream over time. It is calculated as the area under the plasma drug concentration-time curve.
   - **Purpose:** Measures the extent of drug absorption.
   - **Calculation:**

- **AUC^0-t:** Area under the curve from time zero to the last measurable concentration.
- **AUC^0-∞:** Area under the curve extrapolated to infinity.

  - **Acceptance Criteria:**

    - The 90% confidence interval (CI) for the ratio of the AUC of the test product to the reference product must fall within **80-125%**.

  - **Significance:**

    - Ensures the generic drug delivers the same total amount of active ingredient to the systemic circulation as the RLD.

2. **Cmax (Maximum Plasma Concentration)**

   - **Definition:** The peak concentration of the drug in plasma following administration.
   - **Purpose:** Indicates the rate of drug absorption.
   - **Acceptance Criteria:**

     - The 90% confidence interval (CI) for the ratio of the Cmax of the test product to the reference product must fall within **80-125%**.

   - **Significance:**

     - Confirms that the peak drug levels are comparable, reducing the risk of underdosing or toxicity.

3. **Tmax (Time to Reach Maximum Plasma Concentration)**

   - **Definition:** The time taken to achieve Cmax after drug administration.
   - **Purpose:** Provides additional insights into the rate of absorption.
   - **Evaluation:**

     - Unlike AUC and Cmax, Tmax is not subject to strict numerical criteria but is compared descriptively between the test and reference products.

- **Significance:**

  - Used to evaluate whether the test product achieves therapeutic concentrations at the same rate as the RLD.

Regulatory Criteria for Bioequivalence

1. **Acceptance Range:**

   - The 90% CI for the ratio of test-to-reference product for both AUC and Cmax must be within **80-125%**. This range accounts for biological variability while ensuring therapeutic equivalence.

2. **Highly Variable Drugs (HVDs):**

   - For HVDs (e.g., cyclosporine), scaled average bioequivalence (SABE) is used to widen the acceptance range, often requiring replicate study designs.

3. **Narrow Therapeutic Index Drugs (NTIDs):**

   - For NTIDs (e.g., warfarin, digoxin), stricter BE limits may apply, such as **90-111%** for AUC to ensure patient safety.

Testing Procedures

1. **Study Design:**

   - Typically involves a randomized, crossover study with healthy volunteers.
   - Subjects receive both the test and reference products in two separate periods, with a washout interval in between.

2. **Sample Collection and Analysis:**

- Blood samples are collected at predetermined time points (e.g., 0, 0.5, 1, 2, 4, 6, 8, 12, and 24 hours post-dose).
- Drug concentrations in plasma are measured using validated analytical methods such as HPLC or LC-MS/MS.

3. **Statistical Analysis:**

- Log-transformed PK data are analyzed using ANOVA to calculate the 90% CI for AUC and Cmax.

Factors Influencing Bioequivalence Testing

1. **Drug Properties:**

- Drugs with long half-lives may require parallel study designs to avoid prolonged washout periods.
- Highly variable drugs may necessitate replicate designs to address intra-subject variability.

2. **Formulation Characteristics:**

- Differences in excipients or drug release mechanisms can affect BE outcomes, particularly for modified-release formulations.

3. **Subject Variability:**

- Genetic, metabolic, and physiological differences among participants can influence drug absorption and distribution.

Example Application
Generic Immediate-Release Tablet:

- **Objective:** Compare the test product with the RLD for AUC, Cmax, and Tmax.
- **Results:**

- AUC^0-t Ratio (Test/Reference): 92.5% (90% CI: 85.2–97.8%).
- Cmax Ratio (Test/Reference): 88.9% (90% CI: 81.4–94.7%).

- Tmax: Test product achieves Tmax at 2.5 hours, similar to the RLD at 2.4 hours.

- **Outcome:** Bioequivalence confirmed as AUC and Cmax are within the 80-125% range.

12.4 In-Vitro Tests for Bioequivalence

In-vitro dissolution testing is a widely used surrogate for in-vivo bioequivalence (BE) studies. Regulatory agencies like the FDA and EMA recognize dissolution testing as a critical tool for predicting the in-vivo performance of oral solid dosage forms, particularly for immediate-release (IR) and modified-release (MR) products. This testing method is cost-effective, reproducible, and less ethically complex than human trials, making it a preferred approach in specific cases.

Purpose of Dissolution Testing

1. **Surrogate for In-Vivo Studies:**

   - Dissolution testing simulates the release of the active pharmaceutical ingredient (API) in physiological conditions, predicting how the drug will behave in the human gastrointestinal (GI) tract.

2. **Formulation Development and Optimization:**

   - Identifies differences in drug release profiles between test and reference formulations, helping optimize generic formulations.

3. **Batch Consistency:**

   - Ensures uniformity in drug release between production batches.

4. **Regulatory Submission:**

   - Provides critical data for biowaivers, allowing certain in-vivo BE studies to be waived if dissolution profiles are comparable.

Dissolution Testing Methodology

1. **Dissolution Apparatus:**

   - Conducted using USP-approved apparatus:

     - **Apparatus 1 (Basket):** Suitable for tablets and capsules.
     - **Apparatus 2 (Paddle):** Commonly used for immediate-release formulations.

2. **Media Selection:**

   - Simulates physiological conditions using media like:

     - **Simulated Gastric Fluid (SGF):** pH ~1.2.
     - **Simulated Intestinal Fluid (SIF):** pH ~6.8.
     - Water or buffer solutions covering pH 1.2–6.8 to mimic the GI tract.

3. **Test Parameters:**

   - **Agitation Speed:** Typically 50–100 rpm, depending on the dosage form.
   - **Volume of Media:** Commonly 900 mL.
   - **Temperature:** Maintained at 37°C ± 0.5°C to simulate body temperature.

4. **Sampling Intervals:**

   - Samples collected at regular intervals (e.g., 5, 10, 15, 30, 45, and 60 minutes) to plot dissolution profiles.

5. **Analytical Methods:**

   - Drug concentration in the media is quantified using spectrophotometric or chromatographic techniques like HPLC.

Criteria for Bioequivalence via Dissolution Testing

1. **Comparative Dissolution Profiles:**

- BE is established if the test and reference products show comparable drug release profiles across all sampling points.

2. **Similarity Factor (f2):**

- Used to compare dissolution profiles.
- **Formula:**
  f2=50·log {[1+(1/n)Σt=1n(Rt−Tt)2]−0.5·100}f2 = 50 \cdot \log \{ [1 + (1/n) \sum_{t=1}^{n} (R_t - T_t)^2]^{-0.5} \cdot 100 \}f2=50·log{[1+(1/n)Σt=1n(Rt−Tt)2]−0.5·100}

  - **R_t:** Percent drug dissolved from the reference product at time ttt.
  - **T_t:** Percent drug dissolved from the test product at time ttt.

- **Acceptance Criteria:**

  - f2≥50f2 \geq 50f2≥50: Indicates similarity between test and reference products.

3. **Multimedia Testing:**

- Dissolution profiles are compared in multiple media (e.g., pH 1.2, 4.5, and 6.8) to account for variability in GI conditions.

Applications of Dissolution Testing

1. **Immediate-Release Formulations:**

- Predicts rapid release and absorption of the API, critical for drugs where therapeutic effect depends on quick onset.

2. **Modified-Release Formulations:**

- Ensures controlled or sustained release over a specified time frame.

3. **Biowaivers:**

- In-vitro dissolution testing can replace in-vivo BE studies for BCS Class I (high solubility and permeability) and Class III (high solubility, low permeability) drugs under certain conditions.

Advantages of Dissolution Testing

1. **Cost-Effectiveness:**

   - Eliminates the need for expensive and time-consuming human studies.

2. **Ethical Simplicity:**

   - Avoids the ethical complexities of subjecting volunteers to unnecessary studies.

3. **Reproducibility and Standardization:**

   - Provides consistent and easily reproducible results.

4. **Early Formulation Development:**

   - Aids in identifying formulation problems during development.

Challenges in Dissolution Testing

1. **Complex Drug Formulations:**

   - Modified-release products and combination drugs may exhibit dissolution profiles that are difficult to correlate with in-vivo behavior.

2. **Poor Correlation with In-Vivo Performance:**

   - For drugs with low solubility or permeability (BCS Class II and IV), in-vitro results may not accurately predict in-vivo bioavailability.

3. **Media Selection Issues:**

- Inadequate media may fail to simulate actual physiological conditions.

Example Application
Case Study: Generic Immediate-Release Tablet

- **Objective:** Demonstrate bioequivalence to the RLD using dissolution testing.
- **Method:**

  - Tested using USP Apparatus 2 (Paddle) at 50 rpm in three media: pH 1.2, 4.5, and 6.8.
  - Drug release monitored at 5, 15, 30, 45, and 60 minutes.

- **Results:**

  - Similarity factor (f2) calculated as 55, meeting the regulatory criterion of ≥ 50.
  - Conclusion: Dissolution profiles are comparable, establishing in-vitro BE.

CHAPTER THIRTEEN

Biopharmaceutics Classification System (BCS) and Waivers

13.1 Overview of the Biopharmaceutics Classification System (BCS)

The Biopharmaceutics Classification System (BCS) is a scientific framework developed to classify drug substances based on their solubility and permeability characteristics. It plays a crucial role in generic product development by guiding formulation strategies and enabling biowaivers for certain bioequivalence (BE) studies. Regulatory agencies such as the FDA and WHO have incorporated BCS into their guidelines to streamline the drug approval process and reduce the need for in-vivo BE studies.

Key Components of the BCS

1. **Solubility:**

   - A drug is considered highly soluble if its highest single dose strength dissolves in 250 mL or less of aqueous media across a pH range of 1.2–6.8 at 37°C.
   - Solubility testing ensures that the drug dissolves sufficiently in the gastrointestinal (GI) tract to facilitate absorption.

2. **Permeability:**

   - A drug is highly permeable if its extent of absorption in humans is at least 85%.

- Permeability is assessed using in-vivo studies or in-vitro models, such as Caco-2 cell assays, to predict the drug's ability to pass through the intestinal membrane.

3. **Dissolution:**

- Rapid and complete dissolution is required for certain BCS classifications.
- A drug passes the dissolution criterion if ≥85% of the dose dissolves in 30 minutes in pH 1.2, 4.5, and 6.8 buffers.

BCS Classification Categories

1. **Class I:**

- **High solubility, high permeability.**
- Example: Metoprolol, paracetamol.
- Characteristics: Rapidly absorbed; minimal formulation challenges.
- Biowaivers are frequently granted for IR products.

2. **Class II:**

- **Low solubility, high permeability.**
- Example: Ibuprofen, ketoprofen.
- Characteristics: Absorption is dissolution rate-limited; requires solubility enhancement strategies.

3. **Class III:**

- **High solubility, low permeability.**
- Example: Cimetidine, acyclovir.
- Characteristics: Permeability is the limiting factor; formulation strategies focus on enhancing absorption.
- Biowaivers may be granted with robust dissolution data.

4. **Class IV:**

- **Low solubility, low permeability.**

- ○ Example: Hydrochlorothiazide.
- ○ Characteristics: Poor bioavailability; complex formulation strategies required.

Importance of BCS in Generic Product Development

1. **Streamlining Drug Development:**

   - ○ BCS classification helps predict the challenges in formulation and absorption, reducing trial-and-error approaches in development.
   - ○ Example: Class I drugs with high solubility and permeability allow for faster development due to their predictable absorption profiles.

2. **Regulatory Biowaivers:**

   - ○ For Class I and certain Class III drugs, in-vivo BE studies can be waived if the dissolution profiles of the generic and reference products are comparable.
   - ○ Example: A Class I drug that shows ≥85% dissolution within 30 minutes in multimedia (pH 1.2, 4.5, 6.8) qualifies for a biowaiver.

3. **Cost and Time Efficiency:**

   - ○ Eliminating the need for human studies reduces development costs and timelines, particularly for generic formulations.

4. **Guiding Formulation Strategies:**

   - ○ For Class II drugs, formulation techniques like micronization or salt formation are employed to enhance solubility.
   - ○ For Class III drugs, permeability enhancers or modified release formulations may be explored.

5. **Ensuring Regulatory Compliance:**

   - ○ BCS-guided development aligns with regulatory frameworks, improving the likelihood of product approval.

6. **Improving Patient Accessibility:**

   - By reducing development costs and approval timelines, BCS-driven strategies enable faster access to affordable generics.

Regulatory Framework for BCS

1. **FDA Guidance:**

   - The FDA provides specific criteria for granting biowaivers based on BCS classification.
   - For immediate-release (IR) solid oral dosage forms, biowaivers are permitted for Class I and some Class III drugs under strict dissolution and excipient criteria.

2. **WHO Guidelines:**

   - WHO supports BCS-based biowaivers for essential medicines, promoting global access to affordable drugs.

3. **ICH Harmonization:**

   - ICH guidelines emphasize the role of BCS in fostering international regulatory alignment for drug approval.

Example Applications in Generic Drug Development

1. **Class I Drug (Metoprolol):**

   - Generic development focuses on dissolution testing for biowaivers, bypassing in-vivo BE studies.
   - Simplifies formulation development with minimal excipient modifications.

2. **Class II Drug (Ibuprofen):**

   - Solubility enhancement techniques like salt formation or solid dispersion are used to achieve acceptable dissolution profiles.

3. **Class III Drug (Cimetidine):**

   ◦ Permeability enhancers or advanced delivery systems improve absorption, ensuring therapeutic equivalence.

Challenges in Using the BCS

1. **Limited Biowaiver Scope:**

   ◦ Only Class I and certain Class III drugs are eligible for biowaivers, leaving other categories dependent on in-vivo studies.

2. **Complexity in Permeability Assessment:**

   ◦ In-vitro models may not always accurately predict in-vivo permeability, leading to discrepancies in classification.

3. **Solubility Issues:**

   ◦ For Class II and IV drugs, achieving consistent dissolution across batches can be challenging.

4. **Formulation Impact:**

   ◦ Differences in excipients or manufacturing processes can affect dissolution and absorption, even within the same BCS class.

13.2 BCS-Based Bioequivalence Waivers

BCS-based bioequivalence (BE) waivers are a regulatory provision that allows manufacturers to bypass in-vivo BE studies for certain drug products if specific criteria are met. This approach is particularly valuable for generic drug development, as it reduces the time, cost, and ethical concerns associated with human studies. Regulatory agencies, including the FDA, EMA, and WHO, provide clear guidelines for requesting biowaivers based on the Biopharmaceutics Classification System (BCS).

Criteria for Requesting a BCS-Based Biowaiver

To qualify for a biowaiver, the following criteria must be satisfied:

1. Drug Classification (BCS Class I or Class III)

- **BCS Class I (High Solubility, High Permeability):**

  - Drugs in this class are eligible for biowaivers if they exhibit rapid and complete dissolution.
  - Example: Mctoprolol, paracetamol.

- **BCS Class III (High Solubility, Low Permeability):**

  - Biowaivers are considered if the drug dissolves rapidly and the formulation uses excipients that do not affect permeability.
  - Example: Cimetidine.

2. Solubility Requirements

- A drug is considered highly soluble if:

  - The highest dose strength dissolves completely in 250 mL or less of aqueous media across the pH range of 1.2 to 6.8 at $37°C \pm 1°C$.

- Solubility testing involves:

  - Using multiple pH buffers (e.g., pH 1.2, 4.5, and 6.8).
  - Conducting dissolution studies to confirm rapid dissolution.

3. Permeability Requirements

- For Class I drugs:

  - High permeability is established if at least 85% of the drug is absorbed in humans.
  - Methods to assess permeability include:

    - In-vivo studies with human subjects.
    - In-vitro models such as Caco-2 cell assays.

- For Class III drugs:

- ◦ Permeability is low but must be consistent across formulations to ensure equivalent absorption.

4. Dissolution Testing

- Dissolution criteria for requesting a biowaiver include:

  - ◦ **Rapid Dissolution:** At least 85% of the drug dissolves within 30 minutes in pH 1.2, 4.5, and 6.8 buffers.
  - ◦ **Similarity Factor (f2):** Dissolution profiles of the test and reference products must be similar, with an $f2f2f2$ value ≥ 50.
  - ◦ **Multimedia Testing:** Ensures that dissolution is consistent across a range of pH levels.

5. Excipients Compatibility

- For Class III drugs, the test and reference formulations must contain similar excipients in equivalent amounts, especially those affecting permeability or solubility.
- Examples of excipients to monitor include surfactants, stabilizers, and penetration enhancers.

6. Product Formulation

- The drug product must be an immediate-release (IR) solid oral dosage form.
- Modified-release (MR) formulations are generally not eligible for BCS-based biowaivers.

7. Stability and Quality Assurance

- The drug must demonstrate stability under the intended storage conditions.
- Quality control measures must confirm batch-to-batch consistency in dissolution and other critical parameters.

8. Regulatory Submission Requirements

- To request a biowaiver, manufacturers must submit a detailed dossier, including:

  - Justification for the BCS classification of the drug.
  - Solubility and permeability data.
  - Comparative dissolution profiles of the test and reference products.
  - Information on excipient composition and their potential effects on drug absorption.

Regulatory Guidelines

1. **FDA Guidance:**

   - The FDA's "Guidance for Industry: Waiver of In-Vivo Bioavailability and Bioequivalence Studies" outlines specific requirements for BCS-based biowaivers for IR products.

2. **WHO Guidelines:**

   - WHO supports BCS-based biowaivers to facilitate the availability of essential medicines, particularly in low- and middle-income countries.

3. **EMA Guidelines:**

   - The EMA requires comprehensive data on solubility, permeability, and dissolution for biowaiver applications, particularly for Class III drugs.

Advantages of BCS-Based Biowaivers

1. **Cost and Time Savings:**

   - Eliminates the need for costly and time-consuming in-vivo BE studies.

2. **Ethical Benefits:**

○ Reduces the use of human subjects in clinical trials.

3. **Regulatory Efficiency:**

   ○ Simplifies the approval process for generic drugs, facilitating faster market entry.

4. **Enhanced Access:**

   ○ Encourages the development of affordable generic medicines for global markets.

Challenges in BCS-Based Biowaivers

1. **Limited Scope:**

   ○ Only applicable to Class I and certain Class III drugs, excluding Class II and IV drugs with solubility and permeability issues.

2. **Excipient Concerns:**

   ○ Differences in excipients between the test and reference products can complicate permeability assessments.

3. **Regulatory Stringency:**

   ○ Comprehensive and accurate data are required to satisfy regulatory criteria, increasing the complexity of the application process.

Example Application
Case Study: Metoprolol (Class I Drug)

- **Objective:** Obtain a BCS-based biowaiver for an immediate-release generic tablet.
- **Criteria Met:**

   ○ Solubility: 100 mg dose dissolves completely in ≤250 mL across pH 1.2–6.8.

- ○ Permeability: Human absorption studies confirm ≥90% absorption.
- ○ Dissolution: ≥85% dissolution achieved within 15 minutes in all tested pH buffers.
- ○ Excipients: Formulation contains identical excipients in similar amounts to the RLD.

- **Outcome:** Biowaiver granted, eliminating the need for in-vivo BE studies.

13.3 Case Studies in BCS Waiver Applications

The application of Biopharmaceutics Classification System (BCS) waivers has become a valuable strategy in pharmaceutical development, particularly for generic drug approvals. These case studies illustrate how specific drugs have benefited from BCS-based bioequivalence (BE) waivers, focusing on their solubility, permeability, dissolution profiles, and regulatory compliance.

Case Study 1: Metoprolol Succinate (Class I Drug)
Background:

- **Drug Class:** BCS Class I (high solubility, high permeability).
- **Dosage Form:** Immediate-release (IR) tablet.

Solubility and Permeability:

- **Solubility:** The drug dissolves entirely in 250 mL of aqueous media at pH levels ranging from 1.2 to 6.8.
- **Permeability:** Studies confirmed >90% absorption in humans, classifying it as highly permeable.

Dissolution Profile:

- Comparative dissolution testing in three media (pH 1.2, 4.5, 6.8) showed:

- ○ 85% dissolution within 15 minutes for both the test and reference products.
- ○ Similarity factor $f2f2f2$: 70 (greater than the required threshold of 50).

Outcome:

- BCS-based biowaiver granted due to high solubility, high permeability, and rapid dissolution.
- In-vivo BE studies were waived, saving costs and time.

Significance:

- Demonstrates the simplicity of obtaining a waiver for Class I drugs with rapid and consistent dissolution profiles.

Case Study 2: Cimetidine (Class III Drug)
Background:

- **Drug Class:** BCS Class III (high solubility, low permeability).
- **Dosage Form:** Immediate-release tablet.

Solubility and Permeability:

- **Solubility:** Highly soluble across pH 1.2 to 6.8, with complete dissolution in 250 mL.
- **Permeability:** Low permeability confirmed by human absorption studies, yet consistent across formulations.

Excipients Compatibility:

- Test and reference formulations used identical excipients in similar concentrations, ensuring no effect on permeability.

Dissolution Profile:

- Comparative dissolution in pH 1.2, 4.5, and 6.8 showed:

  - 85% of the drug dissolved within 30 minutes.
  - Similarity factor f2f2f2: 55 (meeting the regulatory threshold).

Outcome:

- Biowaiver granted based on compliance with dissolution and excipient criteria.
- In-vivo BE studies were not required.

Significance:

- Highlights the critical role of excipient compatibility for Class III drugs to qualify for biowaivers.

Case Study 3: Ibuprofen (Class II Drug)
Background:

- **Drug Class:** BCS Class II (low solubility, high permeability).
- **Dosage Form:** Immediate-release tablet.

Challenges:

- **Solubility:** Poor solubility limited the eligibility for a biowaiver.
- **Permeability:** High permeability confirmed in human absorption studies.

Dissolution Profile:

- Comparative dissolution showed significant variability between the test and reference products due to solubility limitations.

Outcome:

- Biowaiver was denied due to non-compliance with dissolution criteria.
- In-vivo BE studies were required to demonstrate bioequivalence.

Significance:

- Emphasizes the challenges faced by Class II drugs in achieving biowaivers due to solubility issues.

Case Study 4: Hydrochlorothiazide (Class IV Drug)
Background:

- **Drug Class:** BCS Class IV (low solubility, low permeability).
- **Dosage Form:** Immediate-release tablet.

Challenges:

- **Solubility and Permeability:** Neither high solubility nor high permeability was achieved, making the drug ineligible for a biowaiver.

Dissolution Profile:

- The dissolution rate was slow and inconsistent across pH levels, further complicating the case.

Outcome:

- In-vivo BE studies were mandatory, and additional formulation efforts were needed to address variability.

Significance:

- Highlights the difficulty of obtaining waivers for Class IV drugs and the need for robust in-vivo studies.

Lessons Learned from BCS Waiver Applications

1. **Class I Drugs:**

   - Represent the ideal candidates for BCS-based biowaivers due to their predictable solubility and permeability.

2. **Class III Drugs:**

   - Biowaivers are feasible with strict control over excipients and rapid dissolution profiles.

3. **Class II and IV Drugs:**

- These classes face significant challenges due to solubility and permeability limitations, often requiring in-vivo studies.

4. Regulatory Alignment:

- Successful applications depend on adhering to regulatory guidelines and providing comprehensive data on solubility, permeability, dissolution, and excipients.

CHAPTER FOURTEEN

Electronic Common Technical Document (eCTD)

14.1 Overview of the eCTD

The Electronic Common Technical Document (eCTD) is an internationally recognized standard for the electronic submission of regulatory information to health authorities. Developed by the International Council for Harmonisation (ICH), the eCTD streamlines the preparation, submission, review, and maintenance of regulatory dossiers, enhancing the efficiency and transparency of drug approval processes.

Definition and Purpose

- **Definition:**
  The eCTD is an electronic format for submitting the Common Technical Document (CTD), a harmonized structure for presenting data required by regulatory agencies for drug approval.
- **Purpose:**

  - To provide a uniform, electronic framework for regulatory submissions.
  - To facilitate the efficient review of applications by regulatory authorities.
  - To ensure compliance with international submission standards.

Key Features of the eCTD

1. **Harmonized Structure:**

    - Based on the CTD format, which consists of five main modules:

- **Module 1:** Regional Administrative Information (specific to each health authority, e.g., FDA, EMA).
- **Module 2:** Common Technical Summaries of Quality, Safety, and Efficacy.
- **Module 3:** Quality Information (Chemistry, Manufacturing, and Controls).
- **Module 4:** Nonclinical Study Reports.
- **Module 5:** Clinical Study Reports.

2. **Electronic Format:**

   - Uses XML backbone for metadata and navigation.
   - Allows hyperlinks and bookmarks for easy navigation.

3. **Lifecycle Management:**

   - Tracks changes across multiple submissions, enabling effective management of amendments and updates.

4. **Global Acceptance:**

   - Supported by regulatory agencies across the United States, Europe, Japan, Canada, and other regions.

5. **Validation Tools:**

   - Ensures submissions meet technical and regulatory specifications through validation software.

Advantages of the eCTD

1. **Standardization:**

   - Provides a consistent framework for regulatory submissions across multiple regions.

2. **Efficiency:**

- Reduces submission preparation time and facilitates faster review by health authorities.

3. **Transparency:**

- Enhances clarity in documentation, enabling reviewers to access required data easily.

4. **Lifecycle Tracking:**

- Simplifies management of regulatory changes, such as variations, updates, and renewals.

5. **Global Alignment:**

- Facilitates simultaneous submissions to multiple regulatory agencies, supporting international market access.

Regulatory Requirements

1. **ICH Guidelines:**

- ICH M4 outlines the CTD structure, while ICH M8 provides specifications for the eCTD format.

2. **FDA Requirements:**

- eCTD is mandatory for New Drug Applications (NDAs), Biologics License Applications (BLAs), and Abbreviated New Drug Applications (ANDAs).

3. **EMA Requirements:**

- The eCTD format is required for all submissions within the European Union.

4. **Health Canada and PMDA (Japan):**

- Both authorities have adopted the eCTD standard for regulatory submissions.

Applications of the eCTD

1. **Drug Approvals:**

   - Used for submitting NDAs, ANDAs, and Marketing Authorization Applications (MAAs).

2. **Post-Approval Changes:**

   - Facilitates the submission of variations, supplements, and amendments.

3. **Renewals and Annual Reports:**

   - Streamlines the submission of periodic updates and renewals.

4. **Clinical Trial Applications (CTAs):**

   - Supports the submission of investigational new drug (IND) applications and clinical trial dossiers.

Challenges in Implementing the eCTD

1. **Technical Complexity:**

   - Requires specialized software and expertise for preparation and validation.

2. **Compliance:**

   - Ensuring adherence to technical specifications and regional requirements can be challenging.

3. **Cost:**

- Initial setup costs for software, training, and resources may be significant for smaller organizations.

Case Study: eCTD Implementation

Scenario: A pharmaceutical company is preparing an ANDA for submission to the FDA.

1. **Preparation:**

   - Modules 1 through 5 are structured using the CTD format, and metadata are added using XML.

2. **Validation:**

   - The submission is validated using eCTD validation software to ensure compliance with FDA requirements.

3. **Submission:**

   - The eCTD dossier is submitted electronically through the FDA's Electronic Submissions Gateway (ESG).

4. **Outcome:**

   - Faster review and approval due to the streamlined eCTD format, enabling timely market entry for the generic product.

Purpose and Structure of the eCTD Submission
Purpose of the eCTD Submission
The Electronic Common Technical Document (eCTD) serves as a standardized, electronic format for submitting regulatory documentation to health authorities. It simplifies the preparation, submission, review, and maintenance of applications for the approval of pharmaceutical products. Below are the primary purposes of eCTD submissions:

1. **Streamlining Regulatory Submissions:**

- Provides a consistent and organized structure for submitting data to regulatory agencies, reducing administrative complexity.

2. **Facilitating Efficient Review:**

- Enables health authorities to access and review regulatory information using advanced navigation features like hyperlinks and bookmarks.

3. **Global Harmonization:**

- Ensures uniformity in submissions across regions by adhering to International Council for Harmonisation (ICH) guidelines.

4. **Lifecycle Management:**

- Tracks updates, amendments, and variations within the same submission dossier, maintaining a clear record of changes.

5. **Cost and Time Efficiency:**

- Reduces the time and resources required for paper-based submissions, ensuring faster approvals.

6. **Regulatory Compliance:**

- Supports adherence to regional and international regulatory requirements, improving the chances of approval.

7. **Facilitating Simultaneous Submissions:**

- Enables companies to submit the same dossier to multiple health authorities worldwide, accelerating global market entry.

Structure of the eCTD Submission

The eCTD format is based on the Common Technical Document (CTD) structure developed by ICH. It comprises five main modules, each serving a specific purpose in the regulatory review process.

Module 1: Regional Administrative Information

- **Purpose:**

  - Contains region-specific administrative and product-related information.
  - Customizable based on the requirements of individual regulatory agencies (e.g., FDA, EMA, CDSCO).

- **Contents:**

  - Application forms.
  - Cover letters.
  - Patent information.
  - Labeling and package inserts.
  - Regional-specific information (e.g., drug master file references, product samples).

Module 2: Common Technical Summaries

- **Purpose:**

  - Summarizes the scientific data provided in Modules 3, 4, and 5.
  - Provides a high-level overview for reviewers.

- **Contents:**

  - Quality Overall Summary (QOS).
  - Nonclinical Overview and Summary.
  - Clinical Overview and Summary.

Module 3: Quality (Chemistry, Manufacturing, and Controls - CMC)

- **Purpose:**

  - Details the quality attributes of the drug substance and drug product, including manufacturing processes and controls.

- **Contents:**

  - Drug substance: Description, characterization, and control strategies.
  - Drug product: Formulation development, manufacturing, and stability data.

Module 4: Nonclinical Study Reports

- **Purpose:**

  - Provides safety data from nonclinical studies conducted in animals or in vitro.

- **Contents:**

  - Pharmacology, pharmacokinetics, and toxicology study reports.
  - Study designs, results, and analyses.

Module 5: Clinical Study Reports

- **Purpose:**

  - Contains data from clinical trials demonstrating the safety and efficacy of the product in humans.

- **Contents:**

  - Study protocols and investigator reports.
  - Efficacy and safety analyses.
  - Clinical pharmacology studies (e.g., bioavailability and bioequivalence).

Structure Highlights

- **XML Backbone:**

  - Facilitates metadata tagging, navigation, and lifecycle management.
  - Enables seamless transitions between different sections and modules.

- **Hyperlinks and Bookmarks:**

  ○ Allow efficient navigation within large volumes of data.

- **Version Control:**

  ○ Tracks changes and updates across submissions to ensure traceability.

Advantages of the eCTD Structure

1. **Clarity and Organization:**

   ○ Ensures that all information is presented in a logical and standardized format.

2. **Efficiency for Reviewers:**

   ○ Simplifies access to specific data points, accelerating the review process.

3. **Flexibility:**

   ○ Adapts to the unique requirements of each regulatory agency while maintaining a global standard.

4. **Lifecycle Management:**

   ○ Facilitates tracking of updates, amendments, and post-approval changes.

Example Application
Scenario: Submission of an Abbreviated New Drug Application (ANDA).

- **Module 1:** Includes FDA-specific forms like Form 356h and patent certification.
- **Module 2:** Provides a summary of bioequivalence studies.
- **Module 3:** Details the generic formulation's manufacturing process and quality attributes.

- **Module 4:** Summarizes preclinical studies for the API.
- **Module 5:** Includes bioequivalence study data for the generic product.

14.2 Modules of the eCTD

The Electronic Common Technical Document (eCTD) consists of five modules, each designed to organize and present specific categories of data required for regulatory submissions. These modules follow the harmonized structure of the Common Technical Document (CTD), ensuring consistency and clarity in the presentation of information to health authorities.

Module 1: Regional Administrative Information

Purpose:

Contains administrative and product-specific information tailored to the requirements of individual regulatory agencies.

Contents:

1. **Application Forms:**

   - Submission-specific forms such as FDA Form 356h, EMA Application Forms, or regional equivalents.

2. **Cover Letters:**

   - Brief overview of the submission, its purpose, and relevant details.

3. **Patent and Exclusivity Information:**

   - Details about intellectual property rights and certifications.

4. **Labeling Information:**

   - Proposed labels, package inserts, and patient information leaflets.

5. **Specific Regional Documents:**

   - Examples: Environmental risk assessments (EU), drug master file (DMF) references, or certificates of pharmaceutical product (CPP).

Key Features:

- Unique to the region where the submission is made.
- Not harmonized under ICH guidelines.

Module 2: Common Technical Summaries
Purpose:
Summarizes the key data from Modules 3, 4, and 5 to provide an overview for regulatory reviewers.
Contents:

1. **Quality Overall Summary (QOS):**

   - High-level summary of the drug's manufacturing, quality control, and stability data.

2. **Nonclinical Overview and Summary:**

   - Summary of pharmacology, toxicology, and pharmacokinetics data from Module 4.

3. **Clinical Overview and Summary:**

   - Summary of clinical trial results, focusing on efficacy and safety (Module 5).

   Key Features:

- Provides concise summaries, facilitating efficient review by health authorities.
- Acts as a guide to the detailed data in subsequent modules.

Module 3: Quality (Chemistry, Manufacturing, and Controls - CMC)
Purpose:
Details the quality attributes of the drug substance and drug product, including manufacturing processes and controls.
Contents:

1. **Drug Substance (API):**

   - Description, characterization, and manufacturing process.
   - Specifications and control strategies for raw materials and intermediates.

2. **Drug Product:**

   - Formulation development, manufacturing processes, and batch records.
   - Specifications for excipients, in-process controls, and finished product testing.

3. **Stability Studies:**

   - Data on long-term, accelerated, and stress stability studies supporting the shelf life.

   Key Features:

- Provides critical data on the physical and chemical quality of the product.
- Essential for ensuring compliance with regulatory quality standards.

   Module 4: Nonclinical Study Reports
   Purpose:
Presents data from animal and in-vitro studies to demonstrate the safety profile of the drug.
   Contents:

1. **Pharmacology Studies:**

   - Mechanism of action, receptor binding, and biochemical effects.

2. **Pharmacokinetics Studies:**

   - Absorption, distribution, metabolism, and excretion (ADME) profiles in nonclinical models.

3. **Toxicology Studies:**

   - Acute, sub-chronic, and chronic toxicity studies.
   - Genotoxicity, carcinogenicity, and reproductive toxicity data.

   Key Features:

- Includes detailed reports, study designs, and results, ensuring transparency in preclinical safety evaluation.

Module 5: Clinical Study Reports
Purpose:
Provides evidence of the drug's safety and efficacy through data from clinical trials in human subjects.
Contents:

1. **Study Protocols and Reports:**

   - Comprehensive details of all clinical studies, including randomized controlled trials (RCTs).

2. **Efficacy Data:**

   - Outcomes demonstrating the drug's therapeutic benefits.

3. **Safety Data:**

   - Reports on adverse events, tolerability, and risk-benefit analysis.

4. **Clinical Pharmacology Studies:**

   - Bioavailability and bioequivalence data for generic drugs.
   - Pharmacokinetics and pharmacodynamics studies.

5. **Post-Marketing Data (if applicable):**

   - Safety and efficacy data collected after product approval.

Key Features:

- Contains pivotal data for regulatory approval, highlighting the drug's clinical utility.

14.3 Preparing a Generic Drug Dossier Using eCTD

Preparing a generic drug dossier in the **Electronic Common Technical Document (eCTD)** format involves organizing data into the structured modules defined by the Common Technical Document (CTD) framework. This approach ensures regulatory compliance, efficient review, and successful approval of the generic product. Below are the key points to include in the submission.

Key Points to Include in Each Module

Module 1: Regional Administrative Information

1. **Application Forms:**

   - Submission-specific forms, such as FDA Form 356h (U.S.) or relevant regional forms.

2. **Cover Letter:**

   - Overview of the submission, product details, and purpose.

3. **Patent and Exclusivity Certifications:**

   - Paragraph IV certifications (for ANDA submissions) if applicable.

4. **Labeling and Packaging Information:**

   - Draft labeling, package inserts, and carton designs consistent with the reference listed drug (RLD).

5. **Regional-Specific Requirements:**

   - Environmental risk assessment (EU), drug master file references, or certificates of pharmaceutical product (CPP).

Module 2: Common Technical Summaries

1. **Quality Overall Summary (QOS):**

   - Concise summary of drug substance and drug product data, including manufacturing processes, specifications, and stability.

2. **Nonclinical Overview:**

   - Brief description of pharmacology, toxicology, and pharmacokinetics from Module 4.

3. **Clinical Overview:**

   - Summarized bioequivalence (BE) study data from Module 5, focusing on efficacy and safety.

Module 3: Quality (Chemistry, Manufacturing, and Controls - CMC)

1. **Drug Substance (API):**

   - Detailed information on the API, including:

     - Manufacturing processes.
     - Characterization data (polymorphism, particle size).
     - Control strategies and specifications.
     - Stability data.

2. **Drug Product:**

   - Details of the generic formulation:

     - Formulation development studies (e.g., excipient compatibility).
     - Manufacturing process description, in-process controls, and batch records.
     - Finished product specifications, including dissolution, assay, and impurity testing.

3. **Stability Studies:**

   - Data from long-term, accelerated, and stress testing, supporting the proposed shelf life and storage conditions.

Module 4: Nonclinical Study Reports

1. **Pharmacology Data:**

   - Mechanism of action, receptor binding, and biochemical pathways (if applicable).

2. **Toxicology Data:**

   - Acute, sub-chronic, and chronic toxicity data for the API.

3. **Pharmacokinetics Data:**

   - Absorption, distribution, metabolism, and excretion (ADME) profiles.

Module 5: Clinical Study Reports

1. **Bioequivalence Study Reports:**

   - Detailed results of bioequivalence testing:

     - Pharmacokinetic parameters (AUC, Cmax, Tmax).
     - Statistical analysis demonstrating equivalence to the RLD.

2. **Clinical Pharmacology Studies:**

   - Reports on pharmacokinetics and pharmacodynamics, if required.

3. **Additional Data (if applicable):**

   - Post-marketing safety data or special studies addressing unique formulation challenges.

Key Considerations in Preparing an eCTD Dossier

1. **Regulatory Compliance:**

   - Ensure all data align with regional and ICH guidelines.
   - Address specific requirements of the target health authority (FDA, EMA, CDSCO, etc.).

2. **Validation:**

   - Use eCTD validation tools to check technical accuracy and ensure proper formatting (e.g., XML backbone).

3. **Lifecycle Management:**

   - Incorporate version control for amendments, updates, and variations.

4. **Consistency with the Reference Product:**

   - Demonstrate pharmaceutical and therapeutic equivalence to the RLD.
   - Match critical quality attributes (CQAs) like dissolution profiles and impurity levels.

5. **Cross-Referencing:**

   - Use hyperlinks and bookmarks for easy navigation between modules.

6. **Data Integrity:**

   - Ensure all raw data, analytical results, and reports are accurate and traceable.

Example Outline for a Generic eCTD Submission

Module	Content
Module 1	Application forms, cover letters, patent certifications, labeling.

Module 2

QOS, nonclinical overview, clinical overview.

Module 3

API details, drug product formulation, manufacturing, stability.

Module 4

Nonclinical pharmacology, toxicology, and ADME data.

Module 5

Bioequivalence study reports, clinical pharmacology studies.

Case Study: Generic Tablet Submission

Scenario:

A company preparing an ANDA for a generic immediate-release (IR) tablet.

1. **Module 1:**

   ◦ FDA Form 356h, Paragraph IV certification, draft labeling.

2. **Module 2:**

   ◦ QOS summarizing formulation and stability.
   ◦ Overview of BE study results.

3. **Module 3:**

   ◦ API specifications (polymorphism, particle size).
   ◦ Drug product data, including dissolution profile matching the RLD.

4. **Module 4:**

   ◦ Nonclinical toxicology and ADME data for the API (previously published or cross-referenced).

5. **Module 5:**

   ◦ Bioequivalence study data showing Cmax and AUC ratios within the 80-125% range.

Outcome:

The eCTD dossier is successfully validated and submitted via the FDA's

Electronic Submissions Gateway (ESG), leading to a faster review process.

CHAPTER FIFTEEN

Quality by Design (QbD) in Generic Product Development

15.1 Introduction to QbD Principles

Quality by Design (QbD) is a systematic approach to pharmaceutical development that emphasizes designing quality into a product and its manufacturing process from the outset. It is a proactive framework endorsed by regulatory agencies like the FDA, EMA, and ICH, ensuring that products consistently meet predefined quality attributes. QbD enhances product understanding, improves efficiency, and reduces regulatory hurdles in generic drug development.

Core Principles of QbD

1. **Quality Cannot Be Tested into a Product:**

   - Emphasizes that quality should be built into the product and process design rather than relying solely on end-product testing.

2. **Product and Process Understanding:**

   - In-depth understanding of the relationship between raw materials, process parameters, and product performance.

3. **Risk Management:**

   - Identifying, evaluating, and mitigating potential risks during development.

4. **Continuous Improvement:**

- Facilitates ongoing enhancements in product quality and manufacturing efficiency.

How QbD Is Applied in Generic Drug Development

QbD is particularly beneficial in the development of generic drugs, where manufacturers must demonstrate equivalence to the reference listed drug (RLD) while optimizing production processes.

Key Elements of QbD in Generic Drug Development

1. Quality Target Product Profile (QTPP)

- **Definition:**
  A detailed outline of the desired quality attributes of the final product.
- **Components:**

  - Dosage form (e.g., tablet, capsule).
  - Strength (e.g., 50 mg, 100 mg).
  - Route of administration (e.g., oral, parenteral).
  - Release profile (e.g., immediate or extended release).
  - Shelf life and stability.

- **Example:**
  For a generic immediate-release tablet, the QTPP may specify:

  - Bioequivalence to RLD within 80-125% confidence interval.
  - Dissolution profile matching the RLD in pH 1.2, 4.5, and 6.8 media.

2. Critical Quality Attributes (CQAs)

- **Definition:**
  The physical, chemical, biological, or microbiological properties that must be controlled to ensure product quality.
- **Examples:**

  - Uniformity of dosage units.
  - Drug release (dissolution rate).
  - Assay (active ingredient content).
  - Impurity levels (related substances).

3. Risk Assessment

- **Tools:**

  - Failure Mode and Effects Analysis (FMEA).
  - Fishbone (Ishikawa) diagrams.

- **Purpose:**

  - Identify and prioritize potential risks affecting CQAs.
  - Develop mitigation strategies.

- **Example:**
  Risk assessment may highlight variability in raw material particle size as a critical factor affecting dissolution.

4. Design of Experiments (DoE)

- **Definition:**
  A statistical approach to study the impact of multiple variables on product quality and process performance.
- **Key Applications:**

  - Optimizing formulation compositions.
  - Identifying critical process parameters (CPPs).

- **Example:**
  DoE may be used to evaluate the effect of binder concentration and granulation time on tablet hardness and dissolution rate.

5. Critical Process Parameters (CPPs) and Critical Material Attributes (CMAs)

- **CPPs:**
  Process parameters that directly affect CQAs, such as mixing time, compression force, or drying temperature.
- **CMAs:**
  Attributes of raw materials that influence CQAs, such as particle size,

flowability, and moisture content.

- **Example:**
In a wet granulation process, granulation speed and binder viscosity may be identified as CPPs.

6. Control Strategy

- **Definition:**
A planned set of controls derived from QTPP, CQAs, CPPs, and CMAs to ensure consistent product quality.
- **Types of Controls:**

  ◦ Raw material specifications.
  ◦ In-process controls (e.g., blend uniformity testing).
  ◦ Final product testing (e.g., assay and dissolution).

- **Example:**
Real-time monitoring of granule size using Process Analytical Technology (PAT).

7. Continuous Monitoring and Improvement

- **Purpose:**

  ◦ Use real-time data to ensure process consistency and improve efficiency.
  ◦ Support post-approval changes without extensive regulatory submissions.

- **Example:**
Implementing PAT tools for continuous monitoring of blending uniformity in real-time.

Benefits of QbD in Generic Drug Development

1. **Regulatory Compliance:**

- Aligns with ICH Q8, Q9, and Q10 guidelines, ensuring smoother regulatory approvals.

2. **Enhanced Product Quality:**

- Reduces variability and improves consistency across batches.

3. **Cost Efficiency:**

- Optimizes resources by minimizing trial-and-error approaches.

4. **Reduced Time to Market:**

- Accelerates the development process by providing robust data to regulators.

5. **Flexibility in Manufacturing:**

- Allows for adjustments to processes without additional approvals due to built-in quality controls.

Case Study: QbD for a Generic Extended-Release Tablet

1. **QTPP Development:**

- Target dissolution profile matching the RLD over 12 hours.
- Uniform drug release with no dose dumping.

2. **Risk Assessment:**

- Identified compression force and polymer type as critical factors affecting drug release.

3. **DoE Application:**

- Studied the effect of polymer concentration and granulation method on dissolution.

4. **Control Strategy:**

    ◦ In-process control of tablet hardness and real-time monitoring of coating thickness.

5. **Outcome:**

    ◦ Robust formulation with consistent performance across all batches, facilitating regulatory approval.

15.2 Identifying Critical Quality Attributes (CQA)
Defining Critical Quality Attributes (CQAs) for Drug Products
Critical Quality Attributes (CQAs) are the physical, chemical, biological, or microbiological properties or characteristics of a drug product that must be maintained within predefined limits to ensure its quality, safety, and efficacy. Identifying and controlling CQAs is a fundamental aspect of **Quality by Design (QbD)** in pharmaceutical development.
Characteristics of CQAs

1. **Direct Impact on Product Quality:**

    ◦ CQAs influence the drug's therapeutic performance and stability.

2. **Derived from Quality Target Product Profile (QTPP):**

    ◦ CQAs are identified based on the desired attributes outlined in the QTPP, such as safety, efficacy, and stability.

3. **Subject to Risk Assessment:**

    ◦ Risk assessment tools like Failure Mode and Effects Analysis (FMEA) are used to determine which attributes are critical.

4. **Monitored and Controlled:**

    ◦ CQAs are continuously monitored throughout the manufacturing process to ensure compliance.

Examples of Common CQAs

1. **Physical Attributes:**

   - Particle size and distribution.
   - Tablet hardness, friability, and thickness.
   - Uniformity of dosage form.

2. **Chemical Attributes:**

   - Assay (active ingredient content).
   - Impurity levels, including degradation products.
   - pH and osmolarity for liquid formulations.

3. **Biological Attributes:**

   - Sterility and microbial limits.
   - Endotoxin levels in injectables.

4. **Performance Attributes:**

   - Dissolution rate and profile.
   - Disintegration time.
   - Release kinetics for modified-release formulations.

Steps to Identify CQAs
1. Define the Quality Target Product Profile (QTPP):

- Outline the desired characteristics of the drug product, such as dosage form, strength, and release profile.

2. Conduct Risk Assessment:

- Use risk assessment tools to evaluate how various attributes impact product quality.
- Focus on attributes that directly influence safety, efficacy, or stability.

3. Analyze Formulation and Process Variables:

- Identify material attributes (e.g., API particle size, excipient properties) and process parameters (e.g., mixing speed, drying time) that affect CQAs.

4. Perform Experimental Studies:

- Use Design of Experiments (DoE) to understand the relationship between CQAs and manufacturing processes.

5. Establish Control Limits:

- Define acceptable ranges for each CQA based on experimental data and regulatory requirements.

Defining CQAs for Specific Dosage Forms
1. Solid Oral Dosage Forms (e.g., Tablets, Capsules):

- **CQAs:**

  - Particle size distribution of the API.
  - Blend uniformity.
  - Tablet hardness, friability, and thickness.
  - Dissolution rate and disintegration time.

- **Impact:**

  - Affects bioavailability, stability, and patient compliance.

2. Injectable Products:

- **CQAs:**

  - Sterility and endotoxin levels.
  - Osmolarity and pH.
  - Assay and impurity levels.

- **Impact:**

- Ensures safety (e.g., absence of microbial contamination) and efficacy.

3. Modified-Release Formulations:

- **CQAs:**

  - Coating thickness for tablets.
  - Polymer type and concentration.
  - Drug release profile over time.

- **Impact:**

  - Maintains consistent drug release, preventing dose dumping.

4. Topical Products:

- **CQAs:**

  - Viscosity and spreadability.
  - Assay of active ingredient.
  - Particle size for suspension-based formulations.

- **Impact:**

  - Influences ease of application and therapeutic effect.

Case Study: CQAs for a Generic Immediate-Release Tablet

1. **QTPP:**

   - Match the dissolution profile of the reference listed drug (RLD) in pH 1.2, 4.5, and 6.8 media.
   - Ensure uniformity of dosage units and assay.

2. **Identified CQAs:**

   - API particle size: Impacts dissolution rate.

- ◦ Blend uniformity: Ensures consistent content in each tablet.
- ◦ Dissolution rate: Directly affects bioequivalence to the RLD.
- ◦ Hardness and friability: Impacts mechanical integrity and patient compliance.

3. **Control Strategy:**

- ◦ Implement real-time monitoring of blend uniformity.
- ◦ Use validated methods to measure dissolution at multiple time points.

Regulatory Perspective on CQAs

1. **ICH Q8 (R2):**

- ◦ Emphasizes the identification and control of CQAs as part of pharmaceutical development.

2. **FDA Guidance:**

- ◦ Requires detailed documentation of CQAs in regulatory submissions, particularly for ANDAs and NDAs.

3. **Global Harmonization:**

- ◦ Regulatory agencies worldwide align their guidelines on CQAs, ensuring consistent quality standards.

Benefits of Identifying CQAs

1. **Enhanced Product Quality:**

- ◦ Reduces variability and ensures consistent performance.

2. **Regulatory Compliance:**

- ◦ Aligns with global guidelines, facilitating faster approvals.

3. **Risk Mitigation:**

- Proactively addresses potential issues, reducing product recalls.

4. Cost Efficiency:

- Streamlines manufacturing processes, reducing waste.

15.3 Implementing QbD in Formulation and Process Development
Introduction to QbD Implementation

Quality by Design (QbD) in formulation and process development involves a systematic, science-driven approach to design quality into a pharmaceutical product. By leveraging tools such as Design of Experiments (DoE), QbD enables manufacturers to gain a deeper understanding of the relationships between formulation components, manufacturing processes, and product quality. This ensures consistent quality, regulatory compliance, and improved efficiency.

Steps in Implementing QbD

1. **Define the Quality Target Product Profile (QTPP):**

   - Establish the desired product characteristics, including dosage form, strength, and therapeutic efficacy.

2. **Identify Critical Quality Attributes (CQAs):**

   - Determine which physical, chemical, or biological properties of the product must be controlled to meet the QTPP.

3. **Assess Risks:**

   - Use risk assessment tools to prioritize factors that may impact CQAs, such as material attributes and process parameters.

4. **Apply Design of Experiments (DoE):**

   - Conduct systematic studies to evaluate the effects of formulation and process variables on CQAs.

5. **Develop a Control Strategy:**

- Establish robust controls for critical parameters to ensure consistent quality during manufacturing.

6. **Implement Continuous Monitoring:**

- Use tools like Process Analytical Technology (PAT) for real-time monitoring and continuous improvement.

Role of Design of Experiments (DoE) in QbD
Definition:
DoE is a statistical tool used to study the effects of multiple variables simultaneously, identifying interactions and optimizing processes.
Steps in DoE:

1. **Define Objectives:**

- Identify the formulation or process goal, such as improving dissolution rate or minimizing variability.

2. **Select Factors and Levels:**

- Factors: Variables such as binder concentration, mixing time, or compression force.
- Levels: Specific values for each factor, e.g., low, medium, high.

3. **Choose an Experimental Design:**

- Examples: Full factorial, fractional factorial, or response surface methodology (RSM).

4. **Conduct Experiments:**

- Perform trials based on the selected design matrix, varying factors systematically.

5. **Analyze Results:**

- Use statistical software to evaluate the impact of factors on CQAs and identify optimal conditions.

Applications of DoE in QbD:

1. **Formulation Optimization:**

   - Example: Studying the effect of polymer concentration and granulation method on tablet dissolution.

2. **Process Development:**

   - Example: Optimizing drying temperature and granulation speed for consistent granule size.

3. **Identification of Critical Parameters:**

   - Example: Determining the influence of API particle size and excipient type on blend uniformity.

Key Tools for Implementing QbD

1. **Risk Assessment Tools:**

   - **Failure Mode and Effects Analysis (FMEA):**

     - Identifies and prioritizes potential risks to CQAs.

   - **Fishbone (Ishikawa) Diagrams:**

     - Maps potential causes of variability.

2. **Design of Experiments (DoE):**

   - Optimizes processes by evaluating interactions between multiple variables.

3. **Process Analytical Technology (PAT):**

- ○ Real-time monitoring tools such as spectroscopy for blend uniformity or particle size analysis.

4. **Statistical Process Control (SPC):**

- ○ Tracks and controls process performance over time to ensure consistency.

5. **Control Charts:**

- ○ Monitors key parameters like tablet hardness or dissolution profiles for deviations.

Example: Implementing QbD for a Tablet Formulation
Objective:
Develop a generic immediate-release tablet bioequivalent to the reference listed drug (RLD).

1. **QTPP:**

- ○ Match dissolution profile with the RLD in pH 1.2, 4.5, and 6.8.
- ○ Ensure uniform dosage and stability over 24 months.

2. **Risk Assessment:**

- ○ Identified risks:

  - ▪ API particle size affects dissolution.
  - ▪ Binder concentration impacts tablet hardness.

3. **DoE Application:**

- ○ Factors: Binder concentration, compression force, and granulation method.
- ○ Outcome: Optimal binder concentration and compression force identified for robust dissolution and mechanical integrity.

4. **Control Strategy:**

- Real-time monitoring of compression force during tablet manufacturing.
- Testing each batch for dissolution consistency.

Benefits of QbD Implementation

1. **Enhanced Product Quality:**

   - Reduces variability and ensures batch-to-batch consistency.

2. **Regulatory Compliance:**

   - Aligns with ICH Q8, Q9, and Q10 guidelines, facilitating approval.

3. **Cost and Time Efficiency:**

   - Reduces trial-and-error during development, minimizing resource wastage.

4. **Flexibility in Manufacturing:**

   - Allows post-approval changes with minimal regulatory submissions.

5. **Continuous Improvement:**

Encourages ongoing optimization of product quality and process efficiency

CHAPTER SIXTEEN

Risk Management in Generic Drug Development

16.1 Overview of Risk Management in Pharma

Risk management in pharmaceutical development is a structured approach to identifying, assessing, and mitigating potential risks that may impact the quality, safety, and efficacy of a drug product. It is a critical component of **generic drug development**, where ensuring bioequivalence and maintaining consistent quality are essential to regulatory approval and patient safety.

Importance of Risk Assessment in Development

1. Ensures Product Quality

- Identifies factors that can compromise the critical quality attributes (CQAs) of a drug product.
- Enables proactive control of risks, ensuring batch-to-batch consistency in drug manufacturing.

2. Supports Regulatory Compliance

- Aligns with guidelines such as **ICH Q9: Quality Risk Management**, emphasizing systematic risk identification and mitigation.
- Facilitates smoother regulatory reviews by demonstrating a commitment to quality.

3. Reduces Costs and Time

- Prevents costly errors and delays by addressing potential risks early in the development process.

- Minimizes production downtime and rejections due to quality defects.

4. Protects Patient Safety

- Identifies risks associated with impurities, contamination, or deviations in bioavailability.
- Ensures that the generic product is as safe and effective as the reference listed drug (RLD).

5. Enhances Decision-Making

- Provides a framework for prioritizing critical tasks and allocating resources efficiently.
- Helps in evaluating the impact of process or formulation changes during development.

Key Steps in Risk Management
1. Risk Identification

- **Objective:** Identify potential risks to product quality, safety, or efficacy.
- **Approach:**

  - Brainstorming sessions with cross-functional teams.
  - Using historical data, regulatory guidelines, and scientific literature.

- **Examples of Risks:**

  - Variability in raw material quality.
  - Process deviations during manufacturing.
  - Environmental factors affecting stability.

2. Risk Assessment

- **Objective:** Evaluate the likelihood and impact of identified risks.
- **Tools:**

  - **Failure Mode and Effects Analysis (FMEA):**

- Assesses the severity, probability, and detectability of potential failures.

  - **Fishbone (Ishikawa) Diagrams:**

    - Maps potential causes of issues affecting product quality.

  - **Risk Ranking and Filtering:**

    - Prioritizes risks based on their significance to product CQAs.

- Output:

  - A ranked list of risks, guiding the focus on high-priority areas.

3. Risk Control

- **Objective:** Mitigate high-priority risks to acceptable levels.
- **Approach:**

  - Developing robust control strategies for critical process parameters (CPPs) and material attributes (CMAs).
  - Implementing preventive measures, such as enhanced training or equipment calibration.

- **Example:**

  - For a risk related to API particle size variability, the control strategy could include stricter supplier specifications and real-time particle size analysis.

4. Risk Communication

- **Objective:** Share risk assessment outcomes and mitigation plans with stakeholders.
- **Approach:**

  - Documenting risk management activities in regulatory submissions.

- ◦ Presenting clear action plans to internal teams and regulatory agencies.

5. Risk Review

- **Objective:** Continuously monitor and update risk management plans.
- **Approach:**

  - ◦ Regular reviews during development and post-approval stages.
  - ◦ Adjusting controls based on process performance and emerging risks.

Applications of Risk Management in Generic Drug Development
1. Formulation Development

- **Risk Example:** Incompatibility between API and excipients.
- **Mitigation:** Conducting excipient compatibility studies to prevent stability issues.

2. Process Development

- **Risk Example:** Variability in granule size during wet granulation.
- **Mitigation:** Using Process Analytical Technology (PAT) to monitor granule size in real-time.

3. Stability Testing

- **Risk Example:** Degradation of the drug product under accelerated conditions.
- **Mitigation:** Optimizing formulation and packaging to enhance stability.

4. Manufacturing

- **Risk Example:** Contamination during tablet compression.
- **Mitigation:** Implementing stringent cleaning protocols and environmental controls.

5. Regulatory Submissions

- **Risk Example:** Insufficient data to support bioequivalence.
- **Mitigation:** Conducting robust dissolution and bioequivalence studies aligned with regulatory expectations.

Case Study: Managing Risk in Generic Drug Development

Scenario: Development of a generic immediate-release tablet bioequivalent to the RLD.

1. **Risk Identification:**

    - API variability affecting dissolution rate.
    - Environmental factors impacting tablet stability.

2. **Risk Assessment:**

    - FMEA revealed high severity for API variability.
    - Fishbone diagram identified root causes such as supplier inconsistency and milling process variability.

3. **Risk Control:**

    - Implemented tighter supplier specifications for API particle size.
    - Added real-time monitoring during milling.

4. **Outcome:**

    - Reduced dissolution variability.
    - Achieved bioequivalence with the RLD, meeting regulatory requirements.

16.2 Failure Mode Effects Analysis (FMEA)
Introduction to FMEA

Failure Mode Effects Analysis (FMEA) is a structured and systematic tool used in pharmaceutical development to identify potential risks, evaluate their impact, and prioritize mitigation strategies. It is particularly valuable in generic drug development, where product consistency and compliance with regulatory standards are critical.

FMEA focuses on **failure modes** (ways a process or component can fail), their **effects** (impact on quality), and the **causes** of these failures. By proactively addressing risks, FMEA helps to ensure robust product development and manufacturing processes.

Key Components of FMEA

1. **Failure Mode:**

   - The manner in which a process, system, or component can fail.
   - Example: Deviation in API particle size during milling.

2. **Effect of Failure:**

   - The impact of the failure mode on product quality, safety, or performance.
   - Example: Irregular particle size leading to inconsistent dissolution rates.

3. **Cause of Failure:**

   - The underlying reason for the failure mode.
   - Example: Inadequate equipment calibration or variability in raw material quality.

4. **Severity (S):**

   - The impact of the failure on product quality, safety, or efficacy, rated on a scale (e.g., 1–10, with 10 being most severe).

5. **Occurrence (O):**

   - The likelihood of the failure occurring, rated on a scale (e.g., 1–10, with 10 being highly likely).

6. **Detection (D):**

   - The ability to detect the failure before it impacts the product, rated on a scale (e.g., 1–10, with 10 being least detectable).

7. **Risk Priority Number (RPN):**

   - A numerical value calculated by multiplying Severity (S), Occurrence (O), and Detection (D):

$$RPN = S \times O \times D$$

   - Used to prioritize risks for mitigation.

Steps in Conducting FMEA
1. Assemble a Cross-Functional Team

- Involve experts from formulation, process development, quality assurance, and manufacturing to gain diverse perspectives.

2. Define the Scope

- Specify the process or product being analyzed.
- Example: Wet granulation for tablet formulation.

3. Identify Potential Failure Modes

- List all possible ways the process or system could fail.
- Example: Improper granule size, inadequate binder distribution, or mixing inconsistencies.

4. Analyze Effects of Each Failure Mode

- Determine how each failure mode could impact the product or process.
- Example: Poor granule size distribution could result in tablet friability or low dissolution rates.

5. Assess Causes and Assign Ratings

- Identify the root causes of each failure mode.
- Assign ratings for Severity (S), Occurrence (O), and Detection (D) based on data and expert judgment.

6. Calculate the Risk Priority Number (RPN)

- Rank risks based on their RPN to identify critical areas needing mitigation.

7. Develop Mitigation Strategies

- Implement controls or redesign processes to reduce Severity, Occurrence, or improve Detection.

8. Monitor and Update the FMEA

- Regularly review and revise the FMEA as new data becomes available or process changes occur.

Techniques for Identifying and Mitigating Risks
1. Risk Identification

- Use brainstorming sessions, historical data, and process flowcharts to identify failure modes.
- Tools: Ishikawa (Fishbone) diagrams, Pareto analysis.

2. Risk Mitigation Strategies

- **Design Controls:**

  - Redesign the process or equipment to eliminate the root cause.
  - Example: Use calibrated sieves to control granule size during milling.

- **Preventive Measures:**

  - Implement Standard Operating Procedures (SOPs) for raw material handling.
  - Example: Require suppliers to meet predefined API particle size specifications.

- **Process Controls:**

- Use Process Analytical Technology (PAT) for real-time monitoring.
- Example: Measure granule size during granulation using laser diffraction.

- **Detection Enhancements:**

  - Improve testing methods to detect failures earlier.
  - Example: Use automated blending uniformity analyzers to ensure proper binder distribution.

Example: FMEA for Tablet Compression

Failure Mode
Effect
Cause
S
O
D
RPN

Variability in tablet weight
Dose uniformity affected, leading to therapeutic failure
Inconsistent feed rate during compression
9
7
5
315
Poor granule flow
Tablet defects (capping, lamination)
High moisture in granules
8
6
6
288
Excessive compression force
Reduced tablet dissolution rate
Overcompaction
7
4
3

84

Mitigation Strategies:

1. Implement real-time monitoring of compression force using PAT tools.
2. Optimize drying parameters to maintain granule moisture within acceptable limits.
3. Conduct regular calibration of tablet press feed systems.

Benefits of Using FMEA in Generic Drug Development

1. **Prioritization of Risks:**

   - Ensures that resources are focused on addressing the most critical risks.

2. **Proactive Risk Management:**

   - Identifies and mitigates issues before they lead to product failures.

3. **Improved Process Understanding:**

   - Enhances knowledge of the relationships between process parameters and product quality.

4. **Regulatory Compliance:**

   - Aligns with ICH Q9 and supports robust risk management documentation in regulatory submissions.

5. **Cost Savings:**

   - Reduces losses due to rejected batches, recalls, or delays in development.

16.3 Case Studies in Risk Management

Case Study 1: Risk Management in API Sourcing for a Generic Tablet
Background:

A pharmaceutical company developing a generic immediate-release tablet identified variability in the Active Pharmaceutical Ingredient (API) particle size as a significant risk to product quality, specifically dissolution and bioequivalence to the reference listed drug (RLD).

Risk Identification:

1. API particle size variability affected dissolution rates.
2. Differences in API quality from multiple suppliers posed potential risks to CQAs.

Risk Assessment:

- **Severity (S):** 9 (high impact on dissolution and bioavailability).
- **Occurrence (O):** 7 (moderate likelihood of variability across suppliers).
- **Detection (D):** 5 (limited early-stage detection capability).

Risk Priority Number (RPN): $S \times O \times D = 9 \times 7 \times 5 = 315$.

Risk Mitigation:

1. **Supplier Qualification:**

   - Developed strict API specifications, particularly for particle size distribution.
   - Audited suppliers for consistency in API quality.

2. **Real-Time Monitoring:**

   - Implemented laser diffraction methods for real-time particle size analysis during milling.

3. **Stability Testing:**

   - Conducted accelerated stability studies to evaluate dissolution consistency.

Outcome:

- Ensured consistent dissolution profiles matching the RLD.
- Achieved bioequivalence in the first clinical trial, saving development time and costs.

Case Study 2: Managing Process Variability in Wet Granulation
Background:
During the scale-up of a generic extended-release tablet, inconsistent granule size distribution led to variability in drug release rates.
Risk Identification:

1. Variability in binder concentration affected granule size and tablet compression properties.
2. Inconsistent granule drying caused residual moisture variability, impacting stability.

Risk Assessment:

- **Severity (S):** 8 (moderate impact on release rates).
- **Occurrence (O):** 6 (frequent granulation process variability).
- **Detection (D):** 4 (adequate detection methods available).

Risk Priority Number (RPN): $S \times O \times D = 8 \times 6 \times 4 = 192$.
Risk Mitigation:

1. **Optimized Binder Addition:**

   - Standardized binder addition methods using precise dosing pumps.

2. **Real-Time Process Monitoring:**

   - Introduced Process Analytical Technology (PAT) tools to monitor granule size during granulation.

3. **Controlled Drying Parameters:**

   - Installed moisture sensors to ensure uniform drying.

Outcome:

- Minimized variability in granule size, leading to consistent release rates.
- Successfully scaled up the formulation with no regulatory queries regarding batch reproducibility.

Case Study 3: Addressing Contamination Risks in Injectable Products
Background:
A sterile injectable product experienced contamination due to inadequate environmental controls during manufacturing, leading to multiple rejected batches.
Risk Identification:

1. Non-sterile air supply in the cleanroom environment.
2. Operator errors during aseptic filling.

Risk Assessment:

- **Severity (S):** 10 (direct impact on patient safety).
- **Occurrence (O):** 5 (moderate likelihood with current controls).
- **Detection (D):** 8 (difficult to detect contamination in early stages).

Risk Priority Number (RPN): $S \times O \times D = 10 \times 5 \times 8 = 400$.
Risk Mitigation:

1. **Enhanced Environmental Controls:**

   - Upgraded HVAC systems with HEPA filters.
   - Established stringent air quality monitoring protocols.

2. **Operator Training:**

   - Conducted comprehensive training on aseptic techniques.
   - Implemented gowning procedure audits.

3. **Automated Filling Systems:**

○ Reduced human intervention by introducing automated sterile filling systems.

Outcome:

- Achieved a 95% reduction in contamination-related rejections.
- Strengthened regulatory compliance during facility inspections.

Case Study 4: Stability Risks in Generic Liquid Formulation
Background:
A generic liquid formulation exhibited precipitation of the active ingredient during accelerated stability studies.
Risk Identification:

1. Excipient interactions led to reduced solubility over time.
2. Inadequate pH control during formulation caused precipitation.

Risk Assessment:

- **Severity (S):** 7 (moderate impact on product stability and appearance).
- **Occurrence (O):** 6 (frequent due to unoptimized formulation).
- **Detection (D):** 5 (moderate detection capability during development).

Risk Priority Number (RPN): $S \times O \times D = 7 \times 6 \times 5 = 210$.
Risk Mitigation:

1. **Excipient Compatibility Studies:**

   ○ Conducted preformulation studies to identify compatible excipients.

2. **pH Optimization:**

   ○ Adjusted buffering agents to maintain the product's pH within a stable range.

3. **Accelerated Testing:**

- Modified the formulation and conducted additional stability studies to ensure robustness.

Outcome:

- Resolved precipitation issues, ensuring long-term stability.
- Approved by regulatory agencies with a validated shelf life.

Key Takeaways from Risk Management Case Studies

1. **Proactive Risk Identification:**

   - Using tools like FMEA and Fishbone diagrams helps identify potential risks early in development.

2. **Cross-Functional Collaboration:**

   - Involving formulation scientists, process engineers, and quality assurance teams ensures comprehensive risk management.

3. **Technology Integration:**

   - Adopting advanced tools like PAT and automated systems enhances control and detection capabilities.

4. **Continuous Monitoring and Review:**

   - Regular risk reviews and updates ensure sustained product quality and compliance.

CHAPTER SEVENTEEN

Regulatory Considerations in Generic Drug Development

17.1 Good Manufacturing Practices (GMP) and Good Laboratory Practices (GLP)

Good Manufacturing Practices (GMP) and **Good Laboratory Practices (GLP)** are fundamental regulatory frameworks in pharmaceutical development, ensuring that generic drugs are consistently produced and controlled to meet quality standards. These guidelines are globally recognized and enforced by regulatory authorities such as the **FDA, EMA, and WHO**. Compliance with GMP and GLP is critical for ensuring product safety, efficacy, and regulatory approval.

Regulatory Requirements for GMP

Good Manufacturing Practices (GMP) focus on the manufacturing, packaging, and quality control of drug products. GMP ensures that products are consistently produced and controlled to meet predetermined specifications.

Key Principles of GMP:

1. **Quality Assurance (QA):**

   - Establish systems to prevent contamination, mix-ups, and deviations.
   - Ensure that products meet quality standards for identity, strength, purity, and safety.

2. **Personnel:**

   - Staff must be adequately trained in GMP protocols.
   - Responsibilities must be clearly defined to avoid errors.

3. **Facility and Equipment:**

   - Facilities must be designed to minimize contamination risks.
   - Equipment must be calibrated, validated, and maintained regularly.

4. **Documentation:**

   - Maintain detailed records of manufacturing, testing, and quality control.
   - Implement batch records and Standard Operating Procedures (SOPs).

5. **Process Validation:**

   - Validate manufacturing processes to ensure consistency and reproducibility.
   - Example: Wet granulation validation for tablet production.

6. **Change Control:**

   - Establish procedures to evaluate and approve changes to processes, equipment, or raw materials.

7. **Quality Control (QC):**

   - Perform rigorous testing of raw materials, in-process samples, and finished products.
   - Use validated analytical methods for testing.

Examples of GMP Regulations:

- **FDA's CFR Title 21, Parts 210-211:** Requirements for drug manufacturing and quality control.
- **EMA's EudraLex Volume 4:** EU GMP guidelines for medicinal products.
- **WHO GMP Standards:** International guidelines for pharmaceutical manufacturing.

Regulatory Requirements for GLP

Good Laboratory Practices (GLP) apply to nonclinical laboratory studies that assess the safety and quality of drugs. These studies provide critical data for regulatory submissions, ensuring reliability and reproducibility.

Key Principles of GLP:

1. **Study Design:**

   - Studies must be planned and conducted according to predefined protocols.
   - Protocols should outline objectives, methods, and acceptance criteria.

2. **Personnel:**

   - Staff must be qualified and trained to perform specific tasks.
   - Assign a Study Director to oversee the study.

3. **Facilities:**

   - Laboratories must be appropriately equipped for the intended studies.
   - Separate areas should be designated for storage, testing, and sample preparation.

4. **Documentation:**

   - Maintain detailed records of study protocols, raw data, and final reports.
   - Use secure, tamper-proof systems to manage electronic data.

5. **Sample Handling:**

   - Ensure proper labeling, storage, and tracking of test samples.

6. **Quality Assurance Unit (QAU):**

   - An independent QAU must monitor compliance with GLP standards.
   - Conduct audits and inspections to ensure study integrity.

7. **Archiving:**

  ◦ Retain raw data, specimens, and final reports for regulatory inspection.

Examples of GLP Regulations:

- **FDA's CFR Title 21, Part 58:** GLP standards for nonclinical studies.
- **OECD GLP Guidelines:** International standards for nonclinical testing.
- **WHO GLP Handbook:** Guidance for laboratories conducting safety testing.

Application of GMP and GLP in Generic Drug Development
1. Manufacturing and Process Control (GMP):

- **Scenario:** Production of a generic tablet.

  ◦ GMP ensures consistent blending, granulation, compression, and coating processes.
  ◦ Example: Validate the dissolution profile to match the reference listed drug (RLD).

2. Analytical Method Validation (GLP):

- **Scenario:** Developing and validating a dissolution test.

  ◦ GLP ensures reliable and reproducible methods for evaluating drug release.

3. Stability Studies (GMP and GLP):

- **Scenario:** Conducting long-term and accelerated stability testing.

  ◦ GMP ensures proper storage and handling of samples.
  ◦ GLP ensures accurate and reliable data collection.

4. Bioequivalence Studies (GLP):

- **Scenario:** Nonclinical bioequivalence studies in vitro.

  - GLP compliance ensures data reliability for regulatory submissions.

Importance of GMP and GLP Compliance

1. **Product Safety:**

   - Ensures that drugs are free from contamination, impurities, and variability.

2. **Regulatory Approval:**

   - Noncompliance can lead to delays, rejections, or recalls.
   - Regulatory agencies mandate adherence to GMP and GLP for market authorization.

3. **Data Integrity:**

   - Ensures that all records and results are accurate, traceable, and reproducible.

4. **Consumer Confidence:**

   - Maintains public trust in the safety and efficacy of generic drugs.

Case Study: GMP and GLP Implementation in a Generic Drug Facility
Scenario: A manufacturer developing a generic extended-release tablet.

1. **GMP Compliance:**

   - Validated equipment and processes to ensure uniform drug release.
   - Established SOPs for granulation, compression, and coating.

2. **GLP Compliance:**

   - Conducted dissolution profile testing under GLP standards.
   - Ensured traceability of raw data and results.

Outcome:

- Regulatory submission accepted by the FDA with no observations on manufacturing or testing practices.
- Faster approval due to robust documentation and compliance.

17.2 Regulatory Inspections and Audits
Preparing for FDA and CDSCO Inspections

Regulatory inspections and audits by agencies like the **U.S. Food and Drug Administration (FDA)** and the **Central Drugs Standard Control Organization (CDSCO)** are critical for ensuring compliance with manufacturing, testing, and quality assurance standards. Preparation for these inspections is a rigorous process that requires meticulous planning, thorough documentation, and adherence to regulatory guidelines.

Key Objectives of Regulatory Inspections

1. **Assess Compliance:**

   ○ Verify adherence to Good Manufacturing Practices (GMP), Good Laboratory Practices (GLP), and other regulatory standards.

2. **Ensure Product Quality:**

   ○ Confirm that the processes and facilities meet the required standards for safety, efficacy, and quality.

3. **Verify Data Integrity:**

   ○ Ensure that all records and data are accurate, traceable, and tamper-proof.

4. **Address Observations:**

   ○ Identify deficiencies and provide recommendations for improvement.

Steps to Prepare for FDA Inspections
1. Understand Regulatory Guidelines

- Familiarize the team with FDA's Code of Federal Regulations (CFR) Title 21, Parts 210 and 211 for GMP compliance.
- Review FDA guidance documents specific to generic drug development.

2. Conduct Internal Audits

- Perform mock audits to identify potential gaps in compliance.
- Use checklists that mimic FDA inspection protocols.

3. Review Documentation

- Ensure that all batch records, standard operating procedures (SOPs), and validation reports are complete and up-to-date.
- Maintain logs for equipment calibration, cleaning, and maintenance.

4. Train Personnel

- Conduct training programs to ensure employees are well-versed in their roles during inspections.
- Emphasize proper documentation practices and communication protocols.

5. Maintain Facility Readiness

- Ensure the manufacturing and laboratory facilities are clean, organized, and meet environmental control standards.
- Implement measures to address potential contamination risks.

6. Establish a Response Plan

- Designate a team to address inspector queries and provide required documentation promptly.
- Practice mock interviews to prepare for inspector questions.

Steps to Prepare for CDSCO Inspections
1. Understand CDSCO Guidelines

- Review Schedule M of the Drugs and Cosmetics Act, which outlines GMP requirements in India.
- Familiarize with CDSCO inspection formats and procedures.

2. Conduct Pre-Inspection Audits

- Perform internal audits to assess compliance with Indian GMP standards.
- Evaluate quality control (QC) and quality assurance (QA) processes.

3. Update Documentation

- Ensure alignment of documentation with regulatory requirements, including validation protocols and stability study data.
- Maintain master files and site dossiers in accordance with CDSCO expectations.

4. Implement Continuous Training

- Train staff on Indian regulatory requirements and inspection etiquette.
- Focus on SOP adherence and real-time process monitoring.

5. Address Facility Compliance

- Ensure that cleanrooms, HVAC systems, and storage areas meet CDSCO standards.
- Regularly monitor and record environmental conditions.

6. Establish Inspection Teams

- Assign roles for interacting with inspectors, handling documents, and addressing queries.
- Prepare teams to provide accurate and consistent information.

Key Areas of Focus During Inspections

1. **Documentation:**

- Inspectors review batch manufacturing records, SOPs, QC reports, and training logs for completeness and accuracy.

2. **Facility and Equipment:**

   - Assessments of cleanliness, maintenance, and calibration records for manufacturing and laboratory equipment.

3. **Process Validation:**

   - Verification of validated processes for consistency in production and quality control.

4. **Data Integrity:**

   - Examination of electronic records for compliance with 21 CFR Part 11 (FDA) and equivalent CDSCO requirements.

5. **Deviation and Change Control:**

   - Review of how deviations and process changes are documented, investigated, and resolved.

6. **Stability Studies:**

   - Inspection of stability study data to ensure that the drug's shelf life and storage conditions meet regulatory standards.

7. **Employee Training Records:**

   - Verification of training logs to ensure that all personnel are qualified for their roles.

Handling Inspections
During the Inspection:

1. **Facilitate Transparency:**

- Provide inspectors with requested documents and access to facilities without delays.

2. **Maintain Professionalism:**

   - Ensure staff members are courteous, cooperative, and clear in their responses.

3. **Real-Time Issue Resolution:**

   - Address minor concerns immediately and document corrective actions.

After the Inspection:

1. **Respond to Observations:**

   - Address inspection observations (e.g., Form 483 from FDA) promptly and comprehensively.
   - Provide corrective and preventive action (CAPA) plans with timelines.

2. **Follow Up:**

   - Implement CAPA plans and communicate updates to the regulatory agency.

Common Challenges and Solutions

Challenge	Solution
Incomplete or outdated documentation	Conduct regular audits to ensure documents are current.
Gaps in training	Implement ongoing training programs and refresher courses.
Facility deficiencies	Regularly inspect and maintain facilities and equipment.
Data integrity issues	Use electronic systems with audit trails and tamper-proof logs.

Case Study: FDA Inspection of a Generic Drug Facility

Scenario: A generic drug manufacturer was scheduled for an FDA pre-approval inspection.

1. **Preparation:**

   - Conducted internal audits to identify gaps.
   - Trained employees on responding to FDA queries.
   - Reviewed batch records for bioequivalence batches.

2. **Inspection Findings:**

   - Minor observations related to SOP formatting and storage conditions.

3. **Post-Inspection Actions:**

   - Submitted a CAPA plan to the FDA within the required timeframe.
   - Implemented new SOP templates and updated facility storage controls.

Outcome: Approved for generic drug manufacturing with no major compliance issues.

17.3 Post-Approval Changes and Maintenance of Approval

Introduction

Post-approval changes are modifications made to a drug product or manufacturing process after regulatory approval. These changes may arise due to process optimization, raw material sourcing, manufacturing site changes, or improvements in analytical methods. Regulatory agencies such as the FDA and CDSCO require these changes to be documented and approved to ensure that the drug's safety, efficacy, and quality remain unaffected.

Maintaining approval involves ongoing compliance with regulatory requirements, including updates, periodic reviews, and robust quality management.

Types of Post-Approval Changes

1. Changes to Manufacturing Processes

- **Examples:**

- ◦ Altering granulation methods (e.g., from wet to dry granulation).
- ◦ Modifying equipment used in compression or coating.

2. Changes in Manufacturing Sites

- Examples:

  - ◦ Shifting production to a new facility.
  - ◦ Contracting a third-party manufacturer.

3. Changes in Raw Materials

- Examples:

  - ◦ Changing API suppliers.
  - ◦ Substituting excipients for compatibility or availability reasons.

4. Changes to Packaging

- Examples:

  - ◦ Switching from blister packs to bottles.
  - ◦ Using new packaging materials to improve stability.

5. Changes to Analytical Methods

- Examples:

  - ◦ Updating dissolution test methods.
  - ◦ Switching to more sensitive impurity detection methods.

6. Changes in Labeling

- Examples:

  - ◦ Revising product indications or dosage instructions.
  - ◦ Updating warnings or contraindications.

Regulatory Classifications of Post-Approval Changes
1. Major Changes:

- Require prior approval from regulatory agencies.
- Examples:

  - Change in manufacturing site.
  - Major modification in the formulation.

2. Moderate Changes:

- Require notification to regulatory agencies before implementation (e.g., Changes Being Effected (CBE) submission for FDA).
- Examples:

  - Minor equipment changes.
  - Updates to analytical methods.

3. Minor Changes:

- Require notification to regulatory agencies but can be implemented immediately.
- Examples:

  - Editorial changes to labeling.
  - Minor packaging updates.

Steps to Implement Post-Approval Changes
1. Risk Assessment

- Conduct a detailed evaluation to assess the potential impact of changes on product quality and patient safety.
- Use tools like Failure Mode and Effects Analysis (FMEA).

2. Regulatory Submission

- Prepare and submit a dossier for the change, including:

- ○ Justification for the change.
- ○ Supporting data (e.g., stability studies, validation reports).
- ○ Updated quality and process documentation.

- Follow regional guidelines (e.g., FDA's SUPAC, EMA's variation classification guidelines).

3. Process Validation

- Validate the modified process to ensure consistency and reproducibility.
- Example: Re-validate blending times after switching equipment.

4. Analytical Validation

- Confirm that updated methods produce reliable and reproducible results.
- Example: Validation of new impurity testing methods.

5. Stability Studies

- Conduct studies to evaluate the effect of changes on product stability.
- Example: Testing the impact of a new packaging material on product shelf life.

6. Regulatory Notification

- Submit change notifications to the relevant regulatory authority with the required documentation.

Maintenance of Approval
1. Ongoing Compliance

- Conduct regular internal audits to ensure adherence to regulatory requirements.
- Maintain up-to-date quality documentation and SOPs.

2. Annual Product Reviews

- Evaluate product quality annually to identify trends, deviations, or improvements.
- Compile data on batch performance, stability, and complaints.

3. Periodic Regulatory Updates

- Submit periodic safety update reports (PSURs) as required by regulatory authorities.
- Notify agencies of any significant changes or trends.

4. Inspection Readiness

- Ensure facilities and documentation remain inspection-ready at all times.
- Regularly train staff on regulatory updates and compliance.

5. Post-Market Surveillance

- Monitor adverse event reports and complaints to address safety concerns.
- Implement corrective and preventive actions (CAPA) based on findings.

Case Study: Post-Approval Change in Manufacturing Site
Scenario: A generic drug manufacturer decided to shift production of a tablet formulation to a new facility to increase capacity.

1. **Risk Assessment:**

   - Identified potential risks, including changes in environmental conditions and equipment.

2. **Regulatory Submission:**

   - Prepared a detailed dossier including site information, process validation data, and updated stability studies.
   - Submitted a Prior Approval Supplement (PAS) to the FDA.

3. **Process Validation:**

- Conducted validation batches at the new facility to ensure consistent quality.

4. **Outcome:**

- Regulatory approval granted within six months.

Smooth transition to the new site without impacting product supply

CHAPTER EIGHTEEN

Drug Master File (DMF) and Active Pharmaceutical Ingredient (API) Sourcing

18.1 Understanding the Drug Master File (DMF)

Purpose of DMF in Generic Drug Applications

A **Drug Master File (DMF)** is a confidential, detailed submission to regulatory authorities that provides comprehensive information about the manufacturing, processing, packaging, and storage of drug substances, excipients, or components of drug products. It plays a crucial role in ensuring the quality and consistency of Active Pharmaceutical Ingredients (APIs) and other critical components used in generic drug applications.

Key Objectives of a DMF

1. **Confidentiality for Suppliers:**

   - Protects proprietary information about the manufacturing process while allowing generic drug manufacturers to reference the DMF in their applications.

2. **Facilitating Regulatory Approvals:**

   - Ensures that the quality of APIs and excipients complies with regulatory requirements, thereby expediting the approval process for Abbreviated New Drug Applications (ANDAs).

3. **Standardization and Quality Assurance:**

- Provides consistent information on raw materials and processes, ensuring uniformity in generic drug products.

4. **Regulatory Compliance:**

   - Aligns with global standards, enabling acceptance by regulatory agencies like the **FDA**, **EMA**, and **CDSCO**.

Types of DMFs
DMFs are categorized into five types based on their content:
Type I: Manufacturing Site Information

- Includes general details about facilities, personnel, and manufacturing procedures.
- Rarely used as regulatory agencies prefer site master files for facility details.

Type II: Drug Substance, Drug Substance Intermediate, and Drug Product

- Provides comprehensive details about the API, including:

  - Manufacturing process.
  - Quality controls.
  - Stability data.
  - Packaging details.

- Most commonly referenced type in generic drug applications.

Type III: Packaging Material

- Describes materials used in the packaging of drug products, including:

  - Bottle specifications.
  - Blister pack materials.
  - Container-closure systems.

Type IV: Excipients, Colorants, Flavors, and Materials Used in Drug Preparation

- Includes specifications and quality standards for inactive ingredients.

Type V: FDA Accepted Reference Information

- Used for other types of information not covered under Types I–IV, subject to FDA approval.

Structure and Content of a DMF

A typical DMF includes the following sections:

1. **Cover Letter:**

   - Outlines the purpose and type of DMF submission.
   - Provides a list of authorized parties allowed to reference the DMF.

2. **Administrative Information:**

   - Contact details of the DMF holder.
   - Statement of commitment to update the DMF regularly.

3. **Technical Information:**

   - Comprehensive details about the manufacturing process, including:

     - Raw material specifications.
     - Manufacturing flow charts.
     - Critical process parameters (CPPs) and controls.

   - Analytical methods and validation reports.
   - Stability study protocols and results.

4. **Confidentiality Statement:**

   - Asserts the proprietary nature of the information provided.

Role of DMFs in Generic Drug Applications

1. **API Quality Assurance:**

   - A DMF ensures that the API meets regulatory quality standards, which is critical for the approval of generic drugs.

2. **Simplifying Regulatory Submissions:**

   - Generic drug manufacturers can reference the DMF instead of submitting detailed API information, saving time and resources.

3. **Regulatory Acceptance Across Regions:**

   - A DMF can be referenced in multiple regulatory jurisdictions, facilitating global market entry for generic drugs.

4. **Alignment with Reference Listed Drug (RLD):**

   - Ensures consistency in the quality of APIs used in generic formulations compared to the RLD.

Regulatory Submissions and Maintenance
DMF Submission:

- The DMF holder submits the file directly to the regulatory agency, such as the FDA.
- A unique DMF number is assigned upon acceptance.

Letter of Authorization (LOA):

- Allows a third party, such as a generic drug manufacturer, to reference the DMF in their ANDA or NDA without accessing proprietary information.

Updates and Amendments:

- DMFs must be updated regularly to reflect any changes in manufacturing processes, facilities, or controls.

Annual Reports:

- Most regulatory agencies, including the FDA, require annual updates to confirm the validity and relevance of the DMF.

Case Study: DMF in Generic Drug Development

Scenario: A generic drug manufacturer seeks FDA approval for a tablet formulation using an API from an external supplier.

1. **API Supplier Role:**

   - The supplier submits a Type II DMF to the FDA, detailing the API's manufacturing process, controls, and stability data.

2. **Manufacturer's Role:**

   - The manufacturer includes a reference to the supplier's DMF via a Letter of Authorization (LOA) in the ANDA.

3. **Regulatory Review:**

   - The FDA reviews the DMF for API quality and the ANDA for bioequivalence to the reference listed drug.

Outcome:

- The DMF ensures regulatory compliance for the API, enabling faster approval of the generic drug.

18.3 Quality Control and Assurance for APIs

Introduction

Quality control (QC) and quality assurance (QA) are critical for maintaining the integrity, safety, and efficacy of Active Pharmaceutical Ingredients (APIs) used in drug products. These processes ensure that APIs meet regulatory standards and predefined specifications, preventing inconsistencies and safeguarding patient health. QC focuses on testing and compliance, while QA emphasizes system-wide preventive measures to ensure consistent quality.

Key Objectives of QC and QA for APIs

1. **Ensure Compliance:**

   ◦ Adherence to regulatory requirements such as ICH Q7, WHO GMP guidelines, and FDA standards.

2. **Prevent Contamination:**

   ◦ Maintain strict controls to avoid impurities, cross-contamination, and degradation.

3. **Establish Consistency:**

   ◦ Ensure that every API batch meets the required specifications for quality and performance.

4. **Support Drug Product Quality:**

   ◦ Provide APIs that align with the quality requirements of the finished drug product.

5. **Facilitate Regulatory Approvals:**

   ◦ Provide data that supports regulatory filings, such as DMFs and ANDAs.

Quality Control in API Manufacturing

Quality control involves systematic testing of raw materials, intermediates, and final API batches to confirm that they meet established specifications.

Key QC Activities:

1. **Raw Material Testing:**

- Verify the identity, purity, and quality of raw materials used in API synthesis.
- Example: Testing solvents for moisture content using Karl Fischer titration.

2. **In-Process Controls:**

- Monitor critical process parameters (CPPs) during manufacturing to ensure batch consistency.
- Example: Measuring reaction temperatures and pH levels during synthesis.

3. **Finished Product Testing:**

- Perform physical, chemical, and microbiological tests on the final API.
- Common tests include:

  - Assay (e.g., HPLC for potency measurement).
  - Impurity profiling (e.g., residual solvents and degradation products).
  - Particle size distribution (important for dissolution rate in drug products).

4. **Stability Testing:**

- Conduct long-term and accelerated stability studies to determine API shelf life.
- Example: Monitoring degradation under conditions such as 40°C/75% RH.

5. **Microbial Testing:**

- Ensure that APIs, especially those for parenteral products, meet microbial limit standards.

Quality Assurance in API Manufacturing

Quality assurance focuses on building a robust system to prevent errors, ensure process consistency, and maintain documentation.

Key QA Activities:

1. **Document Control:**

   - Maintain up-to-date SOPs, batch manufacturing records (BMRs), and validation protocols.
   - Example: Controlled document versions to reflect process updates.

2. **Change Control:**

   - Manage changes to raw materials, processes, or equipment with proper evaluation and approval.
   - Example: Assessing the impact of switching API suppliers on quality attributes.

3. **Process Validation:**

   - Validate critical steps in the API manufacturing process to ensure reproducibility.
   - Example: Validating crystallization and drying methods for uniform particle size.

4. **Vendor Qualification:**

   - Audit and qualify suppliers of raw materials to ensure consistent quality.
   - Example: Reviewing the quality systems and processes of a solvent supplier.

5. **Training Programs:**

   - Train personnel in GMP, GLP, and other relevant regulatory standards.

6. **Audits and Inspections:**

- ◦ Conduct internal and external audits to verify compliance with regulatory guidelines.
- ◦ Example: Mock inspections to prepare for FDA or CDSCO site visits.

Critical Quality Attributes (CQAs) for APIs

1. **Identity:**

   - ◦ Confirming that the API is chemically and structurally identical to the intended substance.

2. **Purity:**

   - ◦ Ensuring the API is free from unwanted impurities, such as residual solvents, heavy metals, and degradation products.

3. **Potency (Assay):**

   - ◦ Verifying the active content of the API, typically using methods like HPLC or UV-Vis spectroscopy.

4. **Stability:**

   - ◦ Assessing the API's ability to maintain quality over time under specific storage conditions.

5. **Particle Size Distribution:**

   - ◦ Controlling particle size for APIs intended for solid dosage forms to ensure uniformity in dissolution and bioavailability.

6. **Microbial Limits:**

   - ◦ Ensuring compliance with microbial contamination limits, especially for sterile APIs.

Case Study: Ensuring API Quality in a Generic Drug

Scenario: A pharmaceutical company sourcing an API for a generic tablet formulation faced challenges in meeting dissolution profile specifications during batch validation.

1. **Problem Identification:**

   - Variability in API particle size distribution caused dissolution inconsistencies.

2. **Corrective Actions:**

   - Conducted a comprehensive particle size analysis for each batch using laser diffraction.
   - Worked with the API supplier to tighten particle size specifications.

3. **Preventive Measures:**

   - Added particle size as a Critical Material Attribute (CMA) in the quality control plan.
   - Implemented real-time particle size monitoring during milling.

   Outcome:

- Improved dissolution consistency, ensuring bioequivalence with the reference listed drug (RLD).
- Strengthened regulatory compliance and reduced batch rejections.

   Regulatory Standards for API Quality

1. **ICH Q7 Guidelines:**

   - Provide standards for GMP in API manufacturing.
   - Emphasize documentation, validation, and control of impurities.

2. **FDA Guidance:**

   - Mandates comprehensive testing and validation for APIs used in ANDAs and NDAs.

3. **WHO GMP Standards:**

- Outline global expectations for API quality in pharmaceutical products.

4. **Pharmacopoeial Standards:**

APIs must comply with monographs in USP, EP, IP, or JP, as applicable

CHAPTER NINETEEN

Post-Marketing Surveillance and Pharmacovigilance

19.1 Importance of Pharmacovigilance in Generic Drugs

Pharmacovigilance refers to the science and activities related to the detection, assessment, understanding, and prevention of adverse effects or any other drug-related problems. For generic drugs, pharmacovigilance is crucial as it ensures the safety and efficacy of products after they are introduced to the market.

Post-marketing surveillance provides essential data on how the drug performs in real-world scenarios, helping to identify previously unrecognized adverse events and confirming the risk-benefit profile of the product.

Key Objectives of Pharmacovigilance for Generic Drugs

1. **Ensure Patient Safety:**

   - Detect and minimize adverse drug reactions (ADRs) and medication errors that may not have been evident during clinical trials.

2. **Monitor Real-World Performance:**

   - Assess how the generic drug performs in diverse patient populations, including those with comorbidities or taking concomitant medications.

3. **Identify Rare or Long-Term Adverse Effects:**

○ Detect side effects that may occur infrequently or after prolonged use.

4. **Support Regulatory Compliance:**

○ Fulfill regulatory requirements by submitting periodic safety update reports (PSURs) and maintaining an ongoing pharmacovigilance system.

5. **Enhance Trust and Confidence:**

○ Build trust among healthcare professionals and patients by demonstrating a commitment to safety and transparency.

Pharmacovigilance Activities in Generic Drugs
1. Adverse Event Reporting:

- Collect reports of adverse drug reactions (ADRs) from healthcare providers, patients, and distributors.
- Use structured reporting systems such as MedWatch (FDA) and Vigibase (WHO).

2. Signal Detection:

- Analyze collected data to identify potential safety signals, such as unexpected patterns of adverse events.

3. Risk Management Plans (RMPs):

- Develop and implement RMPs to proactively manage and mitigate identified risks.
- Example: Additional monitoring for drugs with narrow therapeutic indices.

4. Periodic Safety Update Reports (PSURs):

- Submit regular safety updates to regulatory agencies detailing adverse events and safety evaluations.

5. Post-Marketing Studies:

- Conduct observational studies or registries to gather long-term safety and efficacy data.

6. Education and Communication:

- Provide training to healthcare professionals on recognizing and reporting ADRs.
- Disseminate updated safety information through bulletins and labeling changes.

Regulatory Framework for Pharmacovigilance
1. FDA Requirements (United States):

- Submission of Individual Case Safety Reports (ICSRs) for serious and unexpected ADRs.
- Maintenance of Risk Evaluation and Mitigation Strategies (REMS) for high-risk drugs.

2. EMA Requirements (Europe):

- Adherence to Good Pharmacovigilance Practices (GVP).
- Establishment of Qualified Persons Responsible for Pharmacovigilance (QPPVs).

3. CDSCO Requirements (India):

- Participation in the Pharmacovigilance Programme of India (PvPI).
- Mandatory adverse event reporting for all marketed drugs.

4. WHO Guidelines (Global):

- Reporting to the WHO Programme for International Drug Monitoring via Vigibase.
- Promotion of harmonized pharmacovigilance practices worldwide.

Case Study: Pharmacovigilance for a Generic Antihypertensive Drug

Scenario: A generic manufacturer launched an ACE inhibitor for hypertension. Within months, reports emerged of angioedema in certain patient groups.

Actions Taken:

1. **Adverse Event Monitoring:**

   - Collected and analyzed data from ADR reports.
   - Identified a higher-than-expected incidence of angioedema.

2. **Signal Evaluation:**

   - Conducted root cause analysis to confirm a link between the drug and the adverse event.

3. **Risk Mitigation:**

   - Updated the product label to include warnings about angioedema risk in certain ethnic groups.
   - Provided educational materials to healthcare providers.

Outcome:

- Improved patient awareness and healthcare provider vigilance reduced the incidence of severe cases.

19.2 Procedures for Monitoring Drug Safety After Approval

Monitoring drug safety after approval is a critical component of pharmacovigilance. It ensures that any adverse effects or safety concerns that were not apparent during pre-market testing are promptly identified and addressed. The process involves systematic collection, analysis, and communication of safety data from various sources.

Key Procedures for Monitoring Drug Safety

1. Adverse Event Reporting

- Collect reports of suspected adverse drug reactions (ADRs) from:

   - Healthcare professionals (e.g., physicians, pharmacists).
   - Patients and caregivers.
   - Distributors and marketing authorization holders.

- Tools: Regulatory reporting systems like FDA's MedWatch or WHO's Vigibase.
- **2. Signal Detection and Evaluation**
- Analyze adverse event data to identify safety signals, which are patterns that may indicate a new or increased risk associated with a drug.
- Techniques:

  - Disproportionality analysis using databases (e.g., EudraVigilance, Vigibase).
  - Statistical methods to compare observed and expected frequencies of ADRs.

- **3. Periodic Safety Update Reports (PSURs)**
- Submit regular reports to regulatory agencies detailing:

  - Adverse event data.
  - Risk-benefit evaluations.
  - Changes in safety information.

- Frequency: Typically every six months to a year for newly approved drugs, and less frequently for older products.
- **4. Risk Management Plans (RMPs)**
- Develop RMPs as part of regulatory submissions to outline measures for identifying, mitigating, and managing risks.
- Components:

  - Safety specifications.
  - Pharmacovigilance activities.
  - Risk minimization measures.

- **5. Active Surveillance Systems**
- Employ structured methods to actively monitor drug safety.
- Examples:

  - Sentinel System (FDA): Uses electronic health records to identify safety issues.
  - Registries: Collect long-term data on specific patient groups or drug classes.

- **6. Post-Marketing Studies**
- Conduct observational studies or Phase IV clinical trials to assess long-term safety and efficacy.
- Examples:

  - Cohort studies to track outcomes in a defined patient population.
  - Case-control studies to identify factors associated with adverse events.

- **7. Labeling Updates and Safety Communications**
- Update product labeling to include new safety information based on post-marketing findings.
- Issue safety communications or advisories to healthcare professionals and the public.
- **8. Pharmacovigilance Audits**
- Conduct regular audits of pharmacovigilance systems to ensure compliance with regulatory standards.

19.3 Case Studies in Post-Marketing Surveillance

Case Study 1: Withdrawn NSAID Due to Cardiovascular Risk

Scenario: A nonsteroidal anti-inflammatory drug (NSAID) was approved and widely used for pain management. Post-marketing surveillance revealed an increased risk of cardiovascular events.

Actions Taken:

- **Signal Detection:**

  - Analysis of spontaneous reports indicated a higher frequency of heart attacks in patients using the drug.
  - Data from large-scale observational studies confirmed the risk.

- **Regulatory Response:**

  - The FDA and EMA required updated labeling to warn about cardiovascular risks.
  - The manufacturer conducted additional clinical studies to assess the drug's safety profile.

- **Outcome:**

- ◦ Due to continued reports and emerging evidence, the drug was eventually withdrawn from the market.

- **Case Study 2: Labeling Update for Antiepileptic Drug**
  Scenario: An antiepileptic drug showed evidence of an increased risk of suicidal ideation in post-marketing studies.
  Actions Taken:
- **Data Analysis:**

  - ◦ Adverse event reports and meta-analyses of clinical trials highlighted the risk.

- **Risk Minimization:**

  - ◦ The labeling was updated to include a black box warning about the potential for suicidal thoughts.
  - ◦ Educational materials were provided to healthcare providers to monitor at-risk patients.

- **Outcome:**

  - ◦ Increased awareness and monitoring reduced the incidence of severe adverse outcomes.

- **Case Study 3: Post-Marketing Surveillance for a Generic Drug**
  Scenario: A generic manufacturer launched a bioequivalent version of an anticoagulant. Post-marketing reports suggested differences in bleeding risks compared to the reference product.
  Actions Taken:
- **Root Cause Analysis:**

  - ◦ Investigated potential variability in excipients or formulation.
  - ◦ Conducted additional bioequivalence studies.

- **Regulatory Action:**

  - ◦ The FDA issued a warning letter and mandated additional testing.
  - ◦ The manufacturer revised quality control protocols.

- **Outcome:**

  - Improved manufacturing consistency resolved the issue, and the product remained on the market.

CHAPTER TWENTY

Global Trends and Future of Generic Drug Development

20.1 Emerging Markets for Generic Drugs

20.1.1 Growth of Generics in Emerging Markets

The global demand for **generic drugs** is increasing rapidly, and emerging markets such as **India**, **China**, **Brazil**, **Russia**, and parts of **Africa** are becoming critical players in the pharmaceutical industry. These regions are experiencing significant growth due to various factors such as rising healthcare costs, increasing population, and the need for affordable medication. Generics offer a cost-effective alternative to branded drugs, especially in developing countries where public healthcare funding is limited.

Key Drivers of Growth in Emerging Markets:

1. **Cost Advantage of Generics**: In many emerging markets, the cost of branded medications is prohibitively high for a large segment of the population. **Generics**, which are bioequivalent to their branded counterparts but are sold at a fraction of the cost, provide a practical solution to this problem.

   - **Example**: In **India**, generic medications make up over **70%** of the pharmaceutical market, providing affordable treatments for chronic diseases like diabetes, hypertension, and cancer. Brands such as **Cipla** and **Sun Pharma** dominate the global supply of affordable medications.
   - **Example**: **Brazil**, with its **universal healthcare system**, has integrated generics into its public healthcare programs, helping reduce the costs of essential medicines for chronic conditions such as

hypertension and diabetes.

2. **Patent Expirations**: The expiration of patents for many **blockbuster drugs** has opened opportunities for generic manufacturers to enter the market. In emerging economies, where healthcare budgets are often strained, this has resulted in significant cost savings for governments and patients.

   - **Example**: Drugs like **Lipitor** (atorvastatin) and **Plavix** (clopidogrel) have seen rapid generic adoption in countries like **China** after their patents expired.

3. **Government Support and Regulatory Reforms**: Many governments in emerging markets have recognized the value of generics in reducing healthcare costs and improving access to essential medicines. To support the growth of the generic industry, they have introduced regulatory reforms and pricing policies that incentivize the production and consumption of generics.

   - **Example**: In **China**, the government has implemented the **Volume-Based Procurement (VBP)** program, which negotiates lower prices for generic drugs and prioritizes their use in public healthcare systems. This program has led to a sharp increase in the adoption of generics in China's hospitals and clinics.

4. **Rising Burden of Chronic Diseases**: With growing urbanization and lifestyle changes, emerging markets are facing an increasing burden of chronic diseases such as **diabetes**, **cardiovascular disease**, and **cancer**. These conditions require long-term treatment, making access to affordable generic medications critical for both patients and healthcare systems.

   - **Example**: In **South Africa**, the generic industry plays a vital role in treating the large population of **HIV** patients, where the availability of affordable antiretroviral drugs has been a game changer in public health efforts.

5. **Economic Growth**: As emerging markets continue to experience **economic development**, there is a corresponding increase in healthcare spending. Governments are allocating more resources to improve healthcare infrastructure and provide affordable medications to their populations, which boosts demand for generics.

   ◦ **Example**: In **Mexico**, rising middle-class incomes and expanding health insurance coverage are contributing to increased demand for generics.

20.1.2 Challenges in Emerging Markets

While the potential for growth is significant, there are several challenges facing generic drug manufacturers in emerging markets:

1. **Regulatory Variability**: Regulatory requirements for generics vary widely between countries. Inconsistent approval processes and standards can delay market entry and increase compliance costs for manufacturers.

   ◦ **Example**: In **India**, obtaining regulatory approval for a generic drug may differ significantly from the processes in **Brazil** or **China**, making it difficult for companies to standardize their manufacturing and submission strategies.

2. **Intellectual Property Issues**: In some markets, patent disputes and intellectual property protection can slow down the introduction of generic drugs.

   ◦ **Example**: **India** has faced numerous patent litigation cases from multinational pharmaceutical companies attempting to block the entry of generics for high-value medications like cancer drugs (e.g., **Gleevec**).

3. **Manufacturing Quality**: Emerging markets often face challenges in ensuring that all generic products meet international quality standards. The lack of robust **Good Manufacturing Practices (GMP)** compliance among some manufacturers can lead to recalls and product withdrawals.

◦ **Example**: **Nigeria** has struggled with the issue of counterfeit and substandard medications, which undermines public confidence in generics.

20.2 Future Challenges and Opportunities
20.2.1 Key Challenges Such as Patent Cliffs and Biosimilars

As the generic drug industry grows, it faces both challenges and opportunities that will shape its future. Two of the most significant challenges are **patent cliffs** and the rise of **biosimilars**.

Patent Cliffs:

A **patent cliff** refers to the expiration of patents on blockbuster drugs, which results in the sudden loss of market exclusivity for the original manufacturers. While this presents an opportunity for generic manufacturers, it also creates competitive pressures as multiple generic versions flood the market, driving down prices.

- **Example**: The patent expirations of blockbuster drugs like **Lipitor** (atorvastatin) and **Crestor** (rosuvastatin) led to a sharp decline in sales for the original manufacturers but allowed generics to capture a large portion of the cholesterol-lowering drug market.
- **Challenge**: With fewer blockbuster drugs approaching their patent expiration dates, generic manufacturers may face a slowdown in growth. In addition, the intense competition among generic manufacturers after patent cliffs often leads to price wars, which can reduce profitability.

Biosimilars:

Biosimilars are a relatively new frontier for the generic drug industry. Biosimilars are biologic medicines that are highly similar to already approved **biological drugs** (reference biologics) but are not identical. Unlike traditional small-molecule generics, which are chemically synthesized, biosimilars are derived from living cells and involve complex manufacturing processes.

- **Opportunity**: As patents for major biologics like **Humira** (adalimumab), **Enbrel** (etanercept), and **Herceptin** (trastuzumab) expire, biosimilar manufacturers have the opportunity to enter lucrative markets in therapeutic areas like oncology, autoimmune diseases, and diabetes.

- ○ **Example**: The introduction of **biosimilars** for **trastuzumab** has significantly reduced the cost of treatment for breast cancer patients in Europe and other regions.

- **Challenge**: The development of biosimilars is far more complex and costly than traditional generics. Regulatory approval processes are more stringent, and the manufacturing requires sophisticated facilities that can ensure the **biological similarity** of the biosimilar to the reference product. In addition, the issue of **interchangeability** remains a barrier to widespread adoption.

  - ○ **Example**: In the U.S., regulatory hurdles for establishing biosimilar **interchangeability** (i.e., substituting a biosimilar for its reference product without requiring a physician's approval) remain significant, limiting the uptake of biosimilars compared to Europe, where biosimilar adoption is higher.

20.2.2 Opportunities for Growth

1. **Personalized Medicine**: Advances in **genomic medicine** and **personalized therapies** provide opportunities for the development of generics tailored to specific patient populations or genetic profiles.

   - ○ **Example**: The development of **generic versions** of drugs used in targeted therapies for cancer (e.g., **tyrosine kinase inhibitors**) offers potential for personalized medicine in oncology, where treatments can be designed based on the patient's genetic makeup.

2. **Digital Health and AI**: The integration of **digital health technologies** and **artificial intelligence (AI)** into drug development is creating opportunities for generics to evolve in formulation and delivery methods.

   - ○ **Example**: AI can be used to predict drug interactions, optimize bioequivalence studies, and streamline the drug development pipeline, reducing time-to-market for generic manufacturers.

20.3 Innovations in Generic Drug Development

20.3.1 Technological Advances (3D Printing, Nanotechnology)

Technological advancements are reshaping the landscape of generic drug development, providing opportunities to create more **efficient**, **customizable**, and **effective** medications. These innovations are driving new possibilities in how generics are formulated, manufactured, and delivered to patients.

3D Printing of Drugs:

3D printing has emerged as a cutting-edge technology with the potential to revolutionize drug manufacturing. In pharmaceuticals, 3D printing allows for the creation of **precisely tailored dosage forms** that can be customized for individual patients or specific populations. This technology enables the design of **complex drug release profiles**, **multi-drug tablets**, and even **personalized dosing** based on a patient's specific needs.

- **Example:** The **FDA** has already approved **Spritam®**, the first **3D-printed** drug for epilepsy, which offers rapid disintegration and ease of administration. In the future, generic versions of complex medications could benefit from 3D printing technology, allowing for **dose customization** and **simplified production processes.**
- **Opportunity for Generics**: 3D printing could be particularly useful in the development of **generic fixed-dose combinations** (FDCs), where multiple active ingredients are combined in a single tablet. This could be especially beneficial for treating conditions like **HIV/AIDS**, **hypertension**, and **diabetes**, where patients often require multiple medications.

Nanotechnology:

Nanotechnology is another promising area of innovation in generic drug development. Nanotechnology allows for the creation of **nano-sized drug particles** that can improve the **solubility, bioavailability**, and **targeted delivery** of medications. Nanotechnology-based generics can provide more effective drug delivery systems, especially for **poorly soluble** or **unstable** drugs.

- **Example: Abraxane®**, a nano-formulation of **paclitaxel** used in cancer treatment, significantly improves the solubility of paclitaxel and enhances its delivery to tumor cells. While Abraxane is a branded drug, the principles of nanotechnology could be applied to create generic versions of poorly soluble cancer medications or other therapeutics.

- **Opportunity for Generics**: Nanotechnology opens the door for generic manufacturers to create **more effective versions** of existing drugs by improving their **pharmacokinetic profiles**. This can be particularly useful for **oncology drugs**, **antivirals**, or **antibiotics** where targeted delivery can minimize side effects and enhance therapeutic outcomes.

Artificial Intelligence (AI) in Drug Development:

AI is playing an increasingly important role in pharmaceutical research and development, particularly in areas like **formulation design, predictive modeling**, and **clinical trial optimization**. For generic drug manufacturers, AI can help **accelerate the development process**, improve **bioequivalence prediction**, and reduce the costs of bringing generics to market.

- **Example**: AI tools can simulate how a generic formulation will behave in the body, allowing manufacturers to optimize the formulation for **bioequivalence** without needing to conduct multiple iterations of in vivo studies. This can reduce the time and resources required to develop a bioequivalent product.
- **Opportunity for Generics**: AI can also be used in the design of **complex generics**, such as those involving **modified-release formulations** or **drug-device combinations**. By predicting how formulation changes affect drug release and absorption, AI can help manufacturers create more innovative and effective generic products.

Glossary Of Key Terms In Generic Drug Development

1. Abbreviated New Drug Application (ANDA):
The application submitted to regulatory authorities (e.g., FDA) for the approval of a generic drug, demonstrating bioequivalence to the Reference Listed Drug (RLD).

2. Active Pharmaceutical Ingredient (API):
The biologically active component in a drug product responsible for its therapeutic effect.

3. Adverse Event (AE):
Any unintended or harmful effect experienced by a patient following the administration of a drug, regardless of whether it is caused by the drug.

4. Adverse Drug Reaction (ADR):
An unintended, harmful reaction to a drug that occurs at normal doses for treatment, prophylaxis, or diagnosis.

5. Accelerated Stability Testing:
A study designed to speed up the evaluation of a drug's stability by using elevated stress conditions, such as temperature and humidity, to predict shelf life.

6. Bioavailability (BA):
The degree and rate at which an administered drug is absorbed into the systemic circulation, allowing it to reach its intended site of action.

7. Bioequivalence (BE):
A measure showing that two drugs (typically a generic and a reference drug) have similar bioavailability and produce the same therapeutic effects in patients.

8. Biopharmaceutics Classification System (BCS):
A system used to classify drugs based on their solubility and permeability, which helps in determining bioequivalence and waiver for in vivo bioavailability studies.

9. Biologic License Application (BLA):
The submission required to gain FDA approval for the marketing of biological products such as vaccines, blood products, and gene therapies.

10. Biosimilar:
A biologic product that is highly similar to an already-approved reference biologic, with no clinically meaningful differences in terms of safety, purity, or potency.

11. Bracketing and Matrixing Designs:
Approaches used in stability testing to reduce the number of samples or testing combinations, while still providing reliable stability data.

12. Certificate of Analysis (CoA):
A document provided by the API or excipient manufacturer that certifies the quality and purity of a substance, based on analytical testing results.

13. Chemistry, Manufacturing, and Controls (CMC):
A section of a drug application that outlines the processes and controls used in the drug's manufacture, ensuring product quality.

14. Cleanroom:
A controlled environment with low levels of pollutants, used in pharmaceutical manufacturing to ensure sterility and prevent contamination.

15. Clinical Trial:
A research study conducted with human subjects to evaluate the safety, efficacy, and pharmacokinetics of a drug or treatment.

16. Common Technical Document (CTD):
A standardized format for submitting regulatory applications to authorities like the FDA and EMA, containing quality, safety, and efficacy information.

17. Corrective and Preventive Action (CAPA):
A system used to investigate and resolve quality issues in pharmaceutical manufacturing, ensuring that corrective measures are taken to prevent recurrence.

18. Critical Process Parameter (CPP):
A process parameter that must be controlled to ensure the drug product meets its Critical Quality Attributes (CQAs).

19. Critical Quality Attribute (CQA):
The physical, chemical, biological, or microbiological properties that must be controlled to ensure the quality of a drug product.

20. Dissolution Testing:
A laboratory test used to measure how quickly a drug dissolves in a given solvent, which is important for predicting bioavailability.

21. Drug Master File (DMF):
A confidential document submitted to regulatory authorities containing detailed information about the manufacturing, processing, and storage of a drug substance or product.

22. Drug Price Competition and Patent Term Restoration Act:
Also known as the **Hatch-Waxman Act**, this U.S. law established the

generic drug approval pathway through ANDA while balancing the interests of brand-name drug manufacturers.

23. Design of Experiments (DoE):
A statistical method used in process development to study the relationships between multiple factors affecting the outcome of a process.

24. Dosage Form:
The physical form in which a drug is produced and administered, such as tablets, capsules, injections, or suspensions.

25. Drug-Drug Interaction (DDI):
The effect of one drug on the pharmacokinetics or pharmacodynamics of another drug when administered together.

26. Drug Substance:
The unformulated, active component of a drug product, which provides the intended pharmacological effect.

27. Drug Product:
A finished pharmaceutical dosage form that contains the drug substance along with excipients.

28. End-Point Detection:
The method used in titration to determine the point at which the reaction between two solutions is complete.

29. European Medicines Agency (EMA):
The regulatory body in Europe responsible for the scientific evaluation and approval of medicines, including generics.

30. Excipients:
Inactive ingredients in a drug formulation that serve as the vehicle for delivering the active pharmaceutical ingredient (API).

31. Extended-Release (ER):
A dosage form designed to release the drug over an extended period, reducing the frequency of administration.

32. Failure Mode and Effects Analysis (FMEA):
A risk management tool used to identify potential failure points in a process and assess their impact on the product.

33. Finished Dosage Form (FDF):
The final form of a drug product that contains the active ingredient and is ready for administration to patients.

34. First-to-File (FTF):
A status granted to the first generic manufacturer to submit a complete ANDA, giving the company **180 days of market exclusivity**.

35. Food and Drug Administration (FDA):
The regulatory authority in the United States responsible for the approval and oversight of pharmaceutical products, including generics.

36. Formulation:
The composition of a drug product, including the API and excipients, designed to achieve the desired therapeutic effect.

37. Good Clinical Practice (GCP):
An international standard for the ethical and scientific quality of clinical trials, ensuring the protection of participants and reliability of data.

38. Good Laboratory Practice (GLP):
Guidelines governing the conduct of non-clinical laboratory studies to ensure their quality and reliability.

39. Good Manufacturing Practices (GMP):
Regulations that ensure pharmaceuticals are consistently produced and controlled to meet quality standards.

40. High-Performance Liquid Chromatography (HPLC):
An analytical technique used to separate, identify, and quantify components in a mixture, commonly used for drug testing.

41. International Council for Harmonisation (ICH):
An organization that standardizes guidelines for drug development and regulation across different regions.

42. In Vitro:
Experiments or tests performed outside of a living organism, often in test tubes or petri dishes.

43. In Vivo:
Experiments or tests performed within a living organism, such as bioequivalence studies conducted in humans.

44. Investigational New Drug (IND):
A regulatory application submitted to the FDA before conducting clinical trials on a new drug or biologic.

45. Limit Test:
A qualitative or semi-quantitative test to determine whether a particular substance exceeds a specified limit.

46. Long-Term Stability Testing:
Stability studies conducted under standard storage conditions to determine a drug's shelf life and expiration date.

47. Manufacturing Scale-Up:
The process of increasing the production of a drug from laboratory or pilot-

scale batches to full-scale commercial production.

48. Maximum Tolerated Dose (MTD):

The highest dose of a drug that does not cause unacceptable side effects in patients.

49. MedWatch:

The FDA's safety information and adverse event reporting system that allows healthcare professionals and consumers to report issues with drugs and medical devices.

50. Multi-Source Drug:

A drug that is available from multiple manufacturers, typically after the expiration of patent protection for the branded product.

51. Nanotechnology:

The use of nanoparticles in drug formulation to enhance the solubility, bioavailability, or targeted delivery of a medication.

52. New Drug Application (NDA):

The application submitted to the FDA for the approval of a new drug product, which includes clinical trial data on safety and efficacy.

53. No Observed Adverse Effect Level (NOAEL):

The highest dose at which no adverse effects are observed in preclinical toxicology studies.

54. Off-Patent:

A drug that has lost its patent protection, allowing generic manufacturers to develop and market bioequivalent versions.

55. Over-the-Counter (OTC):

Medications that can be purchased without a prescription, often including generic versions of previously prescription-only drugs.

56. Paragraph IV Certification:

A filing by a generic drug manufacturer that claims a patent held by the brand-name drug is invalid, unenforceable, or will not be infringed upon by the generic product.

57. Peak Plasma Concentration (Cmax):

The highest concentration of a drug in the bloodstream after administration.

58. Periodic Safety Update Report (PSUR):

A report that provides an evaluation of the risk-benefit balance of a drug during its post-marketing phase.

59. Pharmacodynamics (PD):

The study of the biochemical and physiological effects of a drug on the body and the mechanisms of drug action.

60. Pharmacokinetics (PK):

The study of how a drug is absorbed, distributed, metabolized, and excreted in the body.

61. Pharmacovigilance:

The process of monitoring and assessing the safety of a drug after it has been approved and is in use, including the reporting of adverse events.

62. Pilot Plant:

A small-scale production facility used to develop and test the manufacturing process before scaling up to full commercial production.

63. Polymorphism:

The ability of a drug substance to exist in more than one crystalline form, which can affect its solubility, stability, and bioavailability.

64. Process Analytical Technology (PAT):

A system for designing, analyzing, and controlling manufacturing processes based on real-time measurements of critical quality attributes.

65. Quality Assurance (QA):

The part of quality management focused on ensuring that all processes and systems meet the required standards for quality.

66. Quality by Design (QbD):

An approach to pharmaceutical development that emphasizes understanding the manufacturing process and controlling variability to ensure consistent product quality.

67. Quality Control (QC):

The testing and verification of the quality of drug products and ingredients at various stages of the manufacturing process.

68. Reference Listed Drug (RLD):

The approved branded drug product to which a generic drug is compared for bioequivalence.

69. Risk Management Plan (RMP):

A document outlining the strategies for identifying, assessing, and mitigating risks associated with a drug product.

70. Risk Evaluation and Mitigation Strategy (REMS):

A program required by the FDA for certain drugs to ensure that the benefits of a drug outweigh its risks.

71. Shelf Life:

The length of time a drug product is expected to remain stable and effective under specified storage conditions.

72. Signal Detection:

The process of identifying potential safety signals from adverse event data collected during post-marketing surveillance.

73. Solubility:

The ability of a drug substance to dissolve in a solvent, which affects its absorption and bioavailability.

74. Specificity:

The ability of an analytical method to measure the drug substance accurately in the presence of impurities, excipients, or degradation products.

75. Spontaneous Reporting System:

A system through which healthcare professionals and patients report adverse drug reactions voluntarily to regulatory authorities.

76. Stability Testing:

The process of testing how long a drug remains stable under various environmental conditions, such as temperature, humidity, and light.

77. Stevens-Johnson Syndrome (SJS):

A severe skin reaction that can be triggered by certain medications, characterized by painful skin lesions and potentially life-threatening complications.

78. Suspected Unexpected Serious Adverse Reaction (SUSAR):

An adverse reaction to a drug that is unexpected, serious, and must be reported during clinical trials.

79. Technology Transfer:

The process of transferring the knowledge and technology required to manufacture a drug from one site (e.g., R&D) to another (e.g., commercial production).

80. Therapeutic Equivalence:

A determination that a generic drug provides the same clinical effect and safety profile as the RLD when used under the conditions specified in the labeling.

81. Therapeutic Window:

The range of drug doses that produce a therapeutic effect without causing significant adverse effects.

82. Time to Maximum Concentration (Tmax):

The time it takes for a drug to reach its maximum concentration in the bloodstream after administration.

83. Toxicology:

The study of the adverse effects of drugs and other chemicals on living organisms.

84. Track-and-Trace:

A system for tracking the distribution of drug products through the supply chain to ensure product authenticity and prevent counterfeiting.

85. Type II Drug Master File (DMF):

A type of DMF that contains detailed information on the API, including its manufacturing, processing, packaging, and storage.

86. Ultrafiltration:

A technique used to separate molecules based on size, often employed in the purification of biological products like biosimilars.

87. Validation:

The process of confirming that a manufacturing process or analytical method consistently produces the desired result within defined parameters.

88. Volume of Distribution (Vd):

A pharmacokinetic parameter that describes the extent to which a drug distributes into body tissues compared to the plasma.

89. World Health Organization (WHO):

An international organization that develops guidelines and standards for drug quality and safety, including for generic drugs.

90. X-ray Diffraction (XRD):

A technique used to determine the crystal structure of a drug substance, which can impact its solubility and stability.

Common Issues In Anda Submissions And How To Resolve Them

The submission of an **Abbreviated New Drug Application (ANDA)** is a crucial step in obtaining regulatory approval for a **generic drug**. However, the process can be fraught with challenges that may lead to delays, additional costs, or even rejections. This appendix outlines some of the most common issues encountered during ANDA submissions and offers strategies to resolve them effectively.

Incomplete or Poor-Quality Bioequivalence Data

Issue:

One of the primary requirements for ANDA approval is demonstrating **bioequivalence** between the generic product and the **Reference Listed Drug (RLD)**. Bioequivalence studies compare the pharmacokinetic properties, such as **Cmax** and **AUC**, of the two products. Common problems include:

- Missing data points
- Poor study design
- Insufficient sample size
- Failure to meet bioequivalence criteria

Resolution:

- **Study Design Optimization**: Ensure that bioequivalence studies are designed according to **FDA** guidelines, with a well-defined **crossover** or **parallel** study design, appropriate dosing intervals, and sufficient sample size.
- **Quality Data Collection**: Ensure that pharmacokinetic data are collected at the correct time points and analyzed using **validated methods**.
- **Reformulation**: If bioequivalence is not achieved, consider reformulating the generic product to improve **dissolution** or **absorption profiles**. For example, adjusting the excipients may help match the release characteristics of the RLD.

Deficiencies in Chemistry, Manufacturing, and Controls (CMC) Section

Issue:

The **Chemistry, Manufacturing, and Controls (CMC)** section of the ANDA is often cited for deficiencies. Common problems include:

- Incomplete or unclear descriptions of the **manufacturing process**
- Insufficient details on **batch-to-batch consistency**
- Lack of robust **stability data**
- Missing information on **excipients** or **API source**

Resolution:

- **Thorough Documentation**: Provide a detailed and step-by-step description of the manufacturing process, including any **in-process controls** and **Critical Process Parameters (CPP)**.
- **Stability Testing**: Ensure comprehensive **stability studies** that follow **ICH Q1A** guidelines, with long-term and accelerated stability data that cover all proposed packaging configurations.
- **Batch Consistency**: Include data from multiple batches (e.g., pilot-scale and commercial-scale batches) to demonstrate consistency in product quality.
- **Source Verification**: Ensure that the **API supplier** has an updated **Drug Master File (DMF)**, and confirm that the excipients used comply with pharmacopeial standards.

Inadequate Impurity Profiling
Issue:

Impurities in the **drug substance** or **drug product** can pose safety concerns and are a frequent reason for ANDA deficiencies. These issues include:

- Failure to identify or quantify all impurities
- Excessive levels of impurities exceeding **ICH Q3A** or **Q3B** thresholds
- Lack of **analytical method validation** for impurity detection

Resolution:

- **Comprehensive Impurity Analysis**: Use validated analytical methods such as **HPLC** or **GC** to detect and quantify impurities, ensuring compliance with ICH guidelines.

- **Batch Testing**: Conduct thorough impurity testing across multiple batches to ensure the drug product meets regulatory limits for **organic, inorganic**, and **residual solvent impurities.**
- **Toxicological Justification**: If impurities exceed ICH thresholds, provide a **toxicological justification** or conduct additional studies to assess the safety of the impurity levels.

Inadequate Stability Data
Issue:
Stability testing issues are common in ANDA submissions, including:

- Insufficient **stability data** (e.g., limited to a short timeframe)
- Failure to conduct tests under both **long-term** and **accelerated conditions**
- Incomplete data for all **packaging configurations** or **strengths** of the drug

Resolution:

- **Comprehensive Stability Studies**: Follow ICH Q1A guidelines to ensure that stability studies cover long-term (e.g., 25°C/60% RH) and accelerated conditions (e.g., 40°C/75% RH). These studies should span a sufficient duration (e.g., **12 months** for long-term stability).
- **Cover All Packaging Configurations**: Ensure that stability testing is conducted on all intended packaging configurations and strengths to demonstrate that the product remains stable across different environments and packaging types.
- **Ongoing Stability Monitoring**: After submission, maintain ongoing stability testing for post-approval batches to confirm long-term product integrity.

Labeling Discrepancies
Issue:
Labeling deficiencies are frequently cited in ANDA rejections, including:

- Inconsistencies between the proposed labeling and the **RLD labeling**
- Failure to meet **FDA labeling requirements**, such as formatting, **font**

size, or safety warnings
- Missing information in **patient information leaflets**

Resolution:

- **Labeling Compliance**: Ensure that the labeling adheres to **21 CFR Part 201** regulations, which govern drug labeling. The generic product's labeling must closely mirror the RLD's labeling in terms of indications, warnings, dosage forms, and administration instructions.
- **Safety Information**: Include all necessary **black box warnings**, contraindications, and usage guidelines. These must match the safety information provided in the RLD labeling.
- **FDA Pre-Approval Consultation**: Use the **FDA's Pre-Approval Labeling Consultation** process to resolve potential discrepancies before submission.

Failure to Meet Dissolution Profile Requirements
Issue:

A common bioequivalence requirement for ANDA approval is matching the **dissolution profile** of the generic drug to that of the RLD. Issues arise when the generic product fails to achieve a similar dissolution rate under the specified testing conditions.
Resolution:

- **Dissolution Method Optimization**: Ensure that the dissolution method follows the FDA's recommended procedures, using appropriate **media**, **pH**, and **apparatus** (e.g., paddle or basket).
- **Reformulation**: If the dissolution profile deviates from the RLD, consider reformulating the product by adjusting the **release mechanisms** or modifying excipients that influence drug solubility.
- **Multimedia Dissolution Studies**: Conduct dissolution testing in different media (e.g., pH 1.2, 4.5, 6.8) to ensure the drug exhibits comparable release characteristics in all conditions.

Patent Litigation and Exclusivity Issues
Issue:

Patent litigation and market exclusivity issues can delay ANDA approval. Problems arise when a generic manufacturer submits a **Paragraph**

IV Certification claiming that the patent for the RLD is invalid, unenforceable, or will not be infringed. Patent holders may file lawsuits to block generic entry, delaying the ANDA approval process.

Resolution:

- **Patent Strategy**: Ensure that a thorough **patent search** is conducted before submitting a Paragraph IV Certification. Collaborate with legal experts to assess the risks of patent litigation.
- **Litigation Preparedness**: Be prepared for patent holders to challenge the Paragraph IV Certification, potentially triggering a **30-month stay** on ANDA approval. Ensure that you have a robust legal team in place to defend the certification.
- **Exclusivity Rights**: If you are the **first-to-file** an ANDA with a Paragraph IV Certification, secure your **180-day market exclusivity** by resolving any patent disputes early and ensuring the ANDA is approvable as soon as the exclusivity period starts.

Inadequate Process Validation

Issue:

Process validation deficiencies, such as incomplete or inadequate validation studies, can lead to concerns about the reproducibility of the manufacturing process and product consistency. Issues may include:

- Failure to demonstrate process reproducibility at **commercial scale**
- Inadequate control of **Critical Process Parameters (CPP)**
- Lack of validation data for **cleaning** and **equipment calibration**

Resolution:

- **Thorough Process Validation**: Conduct process validation studies according to **FDA process validation guidelines**, ensuring that the process is reproducible at both pilot-scale and commercial-scale production. Validate each step of the manufacturing process, including blending, granulation, coating, and packaging.
- **In-Process Controls**: Implement and validate **in-process controls** for all critical steps to ensure batch consistency.
- **Cleaning Validation**: Ensure that cleaning validation is performed to prevent cross-contamination, especially in multi-product facilities.

Insufficient Post-Marketing Surveillance Plan

Issue:

Failure to establish an adequate **pharmacovigilance** or **post-marketing surveillance** plan can lead to ANDA rejection. Regulators require a plan to monitor the safety of the drug after it has been approved and marketed.

Resolution:

- **Pharmacovigilance Planning**: Develop a detailed **Risk Management Plan (RMP)** or **Risk Evaluation and Mitigation Strategy (REMS)** that outlines how post-marketing safety will be monitored and how adverse events will be reported.
- **Adverse Event Reporting System**: Set up a system for collecting, analyzing, and reporting **adverse drug reactions (ADRs)** as part of the post-marketing surveillance strategy.
- **Periodic Safety Updates**: Submit **Periodic Safety Update Reports (PSURs)** to regulatory authorities as required, detailing any safety concerns and steps taken to mitigate risks.

Environmental and Contamination Concerns

Issue:

Environmental contamination or cross-contamination in the manufacturing facility can result in the rejection of an ANDA. Issues such as microbial contamination or poor control over **air quality** and **water systems** can compromise product quality.

Resolution:

- **GMP Compliance**: Ensure full compliance with **Good Manufacturing Practices (GMPs)**, particularly in areas such as air handling, cleanroom operations, and water quality systems. Implement stringent controls to minimize the risk of contamination.
- **Environmental Monitoring**: Establish and validate environmental monitoring programs to regularly assess air quality, particulate matter, microbial contamination, and water purity.
- **Training and SOPs**: Ensure that all staff involved in production follow **Standard Operating Procedures (SOPs)** to minimize human error and contamination risks.

Sample Ectd Submission

Sample eCTD Submission

The **Electronic Common Technical Document (eCTD)** is the standardized format for submitting regulatory documents to authorities like the **FDA, EMA**, and other global health agencies. The eCTD is composed of five modules, and each module contains specific types of documentation required for drug approval, including generic drug applications like ANDAs. This appendix provides a **sample eCTD submission** structure for a **generic drug**, detailing the necessary components of each module.

Module 1: Administrative Information and Prescribing Information

Module 1 contains regional-specific information and does not follow the same standardized structure as the other modules. This section typically includes forms, labeling, and correspondence with regulatory authorities. For the **FDA**, it also includes **REMS** and other risk management documents, where applicable.

Contents of Module 1:

1.1 Forms

- FDA Form 356h (Application to Market a New or Abbreviated New Drug)
- Patent certifications (e.g., **Paragraph IV Certification**)
- User fee cover sheet (for ANDA submissions)

1.2 Cover Letter

- A letter introducing the application and summarizing key points, including a list of enclosed documents.

1.3 Labeling

- Draft labeling, including prescribing information, package insert, and patient information leaflet (PIL).
- Side-by-side comparison of the proposed labeling with the **Reference Listed Drug (RLD)**.

1.4 Risk Management Plans (RMPs) and REMS

- If applicable, submission of the **Risk Evaluation and Mitigation Strategy (REMS)** document detailing plans to manage risks associated with the generic drug.

1.5 **Environmental Impact Assessments** (if required)

- Any environmental assessments (EA) or statements claiming a categorical exclusion under **21 CFR Part 25**.

1.6 **Regional Information**

- Regional-specific information, including information required by the local regulatory authority.

Module 2: Quality Overall Summary (QOS), Nonclinical Overview, and Clinical Overview

Module 2 serves as the bridge between the detailed technical documents in **Module 3** and the broader regulatory summary in **Module 1**. It provides an overall summary of the quality, nonclinical, and clinical sections of the application. For ANDA submissions, the focus is mainly on the **Quality Overall Summary (QOS)**.

Contents of Module 2:

2.1 Table of Contents

- A detailed table of contents for Modules 2 through 5.

2.2 Quality Overall Summary (QOS)

- Summary of the **drug substance** (API): Includes a brief description of the active pharmaceutical ingredient, its characteristics, manufacturing process, control, and stability.
- Summary of the **drug product**: Includes the formulation, manufacturing, and controls of the drug product, along with specifications and analytical methods.
- Summary of impurities: A brief overview of impurity profiles, control strategies, and analytical methods for identifying impurities.
- **Stability summary**: A concise summary of the stability studies conducted, covering both long-term and accelerated testing results.

2.3 Clinical and Nonclinical Overview (if applicable)

- Since ANDA submissions are based on the bioequivalence of the generic drug to the RLD, this section may not include traditional nonclinical and clinical trial data. However, for complex generics or products requiring additional studies, a summary of nonclinical and clinical data may be included.
- **Bioequivalence summary**: A detailed overview of the bioequivalence studies conducted, summarizing the design, results, and key conclusions.

Module 3: Quality (Drug Substance and Drug Product)

Module 3 contains all the detailed information related to the quality of the **drug substance (API)** and **drug product**. This is one of the most important sections for generic drug submissions, as it must demonstrate that the generic drug is of consistent quality, stable, and manufactured under controlled conditions.

Contents of Module 3:

3.1 Drug Substance (API)

3.1.1 General Information

- Nomenclature: Chemical name, generic name, and structure.
- Description of the physical and chemical properties of the API (e.g., solubility, polymorphism).

3.1.2 Manufacturer

- Information on the **API manufacturer**, including the manufacturing site, processes, and Drug Master File (DMF) reference, if applicable.

3.1.3 Characterization

- Evidence of the structure and physical characteristics of the API, including **spectroscopic data** (NMR, IR, etc.) and polymorphism studies.
- Information on impurities, including **genotoxic impurities** and their control.

3.1.4 Control of Drug Substance

- Specification: The quality standards the API must meet (e.g., purity, impurity limits).
- Analytical procedures: Methods used to test the API.
- Validation of analytical procedures: Validation data for the testing methods.

3.1.5 Reference Standards or Materials

- Information on reference materials used in testing the API.

3.1.6 Container Closure System

- Description of the packaging system for the API, including materials and suitability.

3.1.7 Stability

- Detailed **stability data** from long-term and accelerated testing of the API, following **ICH Q1A(R2)** guidelines.
- Shelf life and proposed retest period for the API.

3.2 Drug Product
3.2.1 Description and Composition

- A detailed description of the drug product, including its dosage form, strength, and composition of the finished dosage form.

3.2.2 Pharmaceutical Development

- Explanation of the development of the generic product, focusing on **formulation** and **process development** to ensure bioequivalence to the RLD.

3.2.3 Manufacturing Process Development

- Detailed description of the **manufacturing process**, including flow diagrams and Critical Process Parameters (CPPs).
- **Batch formula** and scale-up considerations.

3.2.4 Control of Excipients

- Specifications and control methods for excipients used in the formulation.

3.2.5 Control of Drug Product

- Final product specifications, including **dissolution profile**, uniformity, and impurity limits.
- Analytical methods and validation reports for the testing of the final drug product.

3.2.6 Container Closure System

- Description of the packaging system for the drug product, including tests for **container integrity** and **compatibility** with the drug product.

3.2.7 Stability

- Detailed **stability data** for the drug product under long-term and accelerated conditions, with a proposed **shelf life** and storage conditions.

Module 4: Nonclinical Study Reports

For generic drug applications (ANDAs), **Module 4** is often minimal or not required, as bioequivalence studies replace the need for extensive **nonclinical (toxicology and pharmacology)** studies. However, for **complex generics** or those with **new formulations**, limited nonclinical data may be necessary.

Contents of Module 4 (if applicable):

4.1 Pharmacology

- Nonclinical pharmacological data, if available or required for complex generics.

4.2 Toxicology

- Toxicology data demonstrating the safety of the generic product. This is typically waived for traditional ANDA submissions.

4.3 Genotoxicity and Carcinogenicity Studies (if applicable)

- Any required studies for evaluating potential genotoxicity or carcinogenicity, particularly for products with new excipients or formulations.

Module 5: Clinical Study Reports

Module 5 contains **clinical data**, including the results of **bioequivalence studies**. Since ANDA submissions do not require full clinical trial data, this section is focused on demonstrating that the generic product is bioequivalent to the RLD.

Contents of Module 5:

5.1 Table of Contents

- A detailed table of contents for the clinical study reports.

5.2 Study Reports of Bioequivalence

- **Bioequivalence study protocol**: A detailed description of the study design, including dosing regimens, subject demographics, and pharmacokinetic endpoints.
- **Study results**: A summary of the key results, including **Cmax**, **AUC**, and **Tmax** values for the generic and RLD products.
- **Statistical analysis**: Detailed analysis of the pharmacokinetic data, demonstrating that the 90% confidence intervals for the ratio of the generic to the RLD fall within the required **80-125% range** for bioequivalence.
- **Adverse event reports**: A summary of any adverse events reported during the bioequivalence study, with an assessment of their severity and relationship to the drug.

5.3 Pharmacokinetic and Pharmacodynamic Studies

- If applicable, additional pharmacokinetic or pharmacodynamic studies demonstrating the bioequivalence of the generic product.

Useful Regulatory Resources

This appendix provides a curated list of important websites, documents, and tools that can be invaluable for generic drug developers. These resources include regulatory agencies, industry organizations, guidelines, and databases that offer essential information and support throughout the generic drug development process.

Regulatory Agencies

1. **U.S. Food and Drug Administration (FDA)**

   - **Website:** www.fda.gov
   - **Description:** The primary regulatory authority in the U.S. overseeing the approval and regulation of pharmaceuticals, including generic drugs.

2. **European Medicines Agency (EMA)**

   - **Website:** www.ema.europa.eu
   - **Description:** The agency responsible for the scientific evaluation and supervision of medicines in the European Union.

3. **Central Drugs Standard Control Organization (CDSCO)**

   - **Website:** cdsco.gov.in
   - **Description:** The regulatory authority in India responsible for drug approval and regulation.

4. **Health Canada**

   - **Website:** www.canada.ca/en/health-canada
   - **Description:** The federal department responsible for health policy in Canada, including the regulation of drugs and medical devices.

5. **World Health Organization (WHO)**

   - **Website:** www.who.int

- ◦ **Description**: An international public health agency that sets global health standards and guidelines, including for pharmaceuticals.

Industry Organizations

1. **Generic Pharmaceutical Association (GPhA)**

   - ◦ **Website**: www.gphaonline.org
   - ◦ **Description**: An organization representing the generic pharmaceutical industry in the U.S., providing advocacy, information, and resources.

2. **Pharmaceutical Research and Manufacturers of America (PhRMA)**

   - ◦ **Website**: www.phrma.org
   - ◦ **Description**: An organization representing the pharmaceutical industry, focusing on drug innovation, research, and development.

3. **International Generic and Biosimilar Medicines Association (IGBA)**

   - ◦ **Website**: www.igbamedicines.org
   - ◦ **Description**: An association representing generic and biosimilar manufacturers globally, promoting the benefits of these products.

Key Regulatory Guidelines and Documents

9. **ICH Guidelines**

   - ◦ **Website**: www.ich.org
   - ◦ **Description**: A comprehensive collection of guidelines for the pharmaceutical industry covering topics such as quality, safety, efficacy, and pharmacovigilance.

10. **FDA Guidance Documents**

    - ◦ **Website**: www.fda.gov/GuidanceComplianceRegulatoryInformation/Guidances
    - ◦ **Description**: Official documents that provide guidance on the FDA's

regulatory requirements, including ANDA submissions and bioequivalence studies.

11. European Medicines Agency Guidelines

- ○ **Website:** www.ema.europa.eu/en/documents/scientific-guideline
- ○ **Description:** A collection of scientific guidelines and recommendations published by the EMA for drug development and approval.

12. FDA Approved Drug Products Database (Orange Book)

- ○ **Website:** www.accessdata.fda.gov/scripts/cder/ob
- ○ **Description:** A searchable database that lists all approved drug products, including information on RLDs, patent status, and exclusivity periods.

Databases and Tools

13. ClinicalTrials.gov

- ○ **Website:** www.clinicaltrials.gov
- ○ **Description:** A database of privately and publicly funded clinical studies conducted around the world, useful for finding information on clinical trials related to specific drugs.

14. Drug Master File (DMF) Database

- ○ **Website:** www.accessdata.fda.gov/scripts/cder/dmf
- ○ **Description:** A database for accessing Drug Master Files submitted to the FDA, providing information on drug substances, excipients, and their manufacturers.

15. FDA MedWatch

- ○ **Website:** www.fda.gov/Safety/MedWatch
- ○ **Description:** The FDA's safety information and adverse event reporting program, providing a platform for reporting adverse events

and safety information related to drugs.

16. **EMA EudraCT Database**

  ◦ **Website**: www.ema.europa.eu/en/clinical-trials/eudract
  ◦ **Description**: A database that provides information on clinical trials conducted in the European Union, including details about trial protocols and results.

17. **PubMed**

  ◦ **Website**: www.pubmed.ncbi.nlm.nih.gov
  ◦ **Description**: A free database of biomedical literature that can provide access to research studies and articles related to generic drugs, bioequivalence, and pharmacovigilance.

Helpful Guides and Resources

18. **FDA Bioequivalence Guidance**

  ◦ **Website**: www.fda.gov/media/71523/download
  ◦ **Description**: A comprehensive guide detailing the FDA's expectations for demonstrating bioequivalence for generic drugs.

19. **WHO Guidelines on Quality Assurance**

  ◦ **Website**: www.who.int/publications/i/item/WHO_TRS_986
  ◦ **Description**: WHO guidelines for good manufacturing practices and quality assurance in the production of pharmaceutical products.

20. **ICH Q10: Pharmaceutical Quality System**

  ◦ **Website**: www.ich.org/products/guidelines/quality/article/quality-guidelines.html
  ◦ **Description**: A guideline outlining the principles of an effective pharmaceutical quality system to enhance product quality throughout the product lifecycle.

1. **ADR** - Adverse Drug Reaction
2. **AE** - Adverse Event
3. **ANDA** - Abbreviated New Drug Application
4. **API** - Active Pharmaceutical Ingredient
5. **AUC** - Area Under the Curve
6. **BCS** - Biopharmaceutics Classification System
7. **BE** - Bioequivalence
8. **BLA** - Biologics License Application
9. **BMR** - Batch Manufacturing Record
10. **CDSCO** - Central Drugs Standard Control Organization
11. **CFR** - Code of Federal Regulations
12. **Cmax** - Maximum Plasma Concentration
13. **CPP** - Critical Process Parameter
14. **CQA** - Critical Quality Attribute
15. **CTD** - Common Technical Document
16. **DMF** - Drug Master File
17. **DoE** - Design of Experiments
18. **EMA** - European Medicines Agency
19. **eCTD** - Electronic Common Technical Document
20. **ER** - Extended-Release
21. **FDA** - Food and Drug Administration
22. **FPP** - Finished Pharmaceutical Product
23. **FMEA** - Failure Mode Effects Analysis
24. **GCP** - Good Clinical Practice
25. **GLP** - Good Laboratory Practice
26. **GMP** - Good Manufacturing Practice
27. **HPLC** - High-Performance Liquid Chromatography
28. **ICSR** - Individual Case Safety Report
29. **ICH** - International Council for Harmonisation
30. **IRB** - Institutional Review Board
31. **LC-MS** - Liquid Chromatography-Mass Spectrometry
32. **LOD** - Limit of Detection
33. **LOQ** - Limit of Quantitation
34. **mAb** - Monoclonal Antibody

35. **MTD** - Maximum Tolerated Dose
36. **OGD** - Office of Generic Drugs
37. **PAT** - Process Analytical Technology
38. **PD** - Pharmacodynamics
39. **PEG** - Polyethylene Glycol
40. **PK** - Pharmacokinetics
41. **PSUR** - Periodic Safety Update Report
42. **QbD** - Quality by Design
43. **QC** - Quality Control
44. **QMS** - Quality Management System
45. **RLD** - Reference Listed Drug
46. **RMP** - Risk Management Plan
47. **REMS** - Risk Evaluation and Mitigation Strategy
48. **RH** - Relative Humidity
49. **SAE** - Serious Adverse Event
50. **SOP** - Standard Operating Procedure
51. **TPD** - Total Packaged Dose
52. **Tmax** - Time to Maximum Plasma Concentration
53. **TRIPS** - Trade-Related Aspects of Intellectual Property Rights
54. **UV-Vis** - Ultraviolet-Visible Spectroscopy
55. **WHO** - World Health Organization
56. **API-MF** - Active Pharmaceutical Ingredient Master File
57. **ART** - Antiretroviral Therapy
58. **BCG** - Bacillus Calmette-Guérin (used in vaccines)
59. **BR** - Batch Record
60. **CAPA** - Corrective and Preventive Action
61. **CEP** - Certificate of Suitability to the Monographs of the European Pharmacopoeia
62. **CMC** - Chemistry, Manufacturing, and Controls
63. **CMS** - Concerned Member State (in EU drug regulation)
64. **CRO** - Contract Research Organization
65. **CT** - Clinical Trial
66. **CTA** - Clinical Trial Application
67. **DCP** - Decentralized Procedure (EU drug approval process)
68. **DRA** - Drug Regulatory Authority
69. **DS** - Drug Substance
70. **DSUR** - Development Safety Update Report
71. **EC** - Ethics Committee

72. **EDQM** - European Directorate for the Quality of Medicines & HealthCare
73. **EMA-CHMP** - European Medicines Agency - Committee for Medicinal Products for Human Use
74. **EMEA** - European Medicines Evaluation Agency (now EMA)
75. **EU** - European Union
76. **FDC** - Fixed-Dose Combination
77. **FTIR** - Fourier Transform Infrared Spectroscopy
78. **GC** - Gas Chromatography
79. **GDP** - Good Distribution Practice
80. **GLIMS** - Global Laboratory Information Management System
81. **HA** - Health Authority
82. **ICH-E6** - International Guideline for Good Clinical Practice
83. **ICP-MS** - Inductively Coupled Plasma Mass Spectrometry
84. **IND** - Investigational New Drug Application
85. **IP** - Indian Pharmacopoeia
86. **IVRT** - In Vitro Release Testing
87. **IVIVC** - In Vitro-In Vivo Correlation
88. **LAL** - Limulus Amebocyte Lysate (test for endotoxins)
89. **LC** - Liquid Chromatography
90. **MAA** - Marketing Authorization Application
91. **MRP** - Mutual Recognition Procedure (EU drug approval process)
92. **NCE** - New Chemical Entity
93. **NDA** - New Drug Application
94. **NDDS** - Novel Drug Delivery System
95. **NIH** - National Institutes of Health
96. **NMT** - Not More Than
97. **NMTT** - Nitroimidazole-Thiol Transport Test
98. **OOS** - Out of Specification
99. **OTC** - Over-The-Counter (non-prescription drugs)
100. **PA** - Prior Approval
101. **PBPK** - Physiologically Based Pharmacokinetic Modeling
102. **PCC** - Pharmaceutical Continuous Manufacturing
103. **PEMF** - Packaging Evaluation Master File
104. **PPI** - Proton Pump Inhibitor
105. **PQ** - Performance Qualification
106. **PQRS** - Prequalification Requirements for Standards
107. **PV** - Pharmacovigilance

108. **PVT** - Process Validation Test
109. **QRM** - Quality Risk Management
110. **RA** - Regulatory Affairs
111. **RSD** - Relative Standard Deviation
112. **RTRT** - Real-Time Release Testing
113. **SDS** - Safety Data Sheet
114. **SFDA** - State Food and Drug Administration (China)
115. **SME** - Small and Medium Enterprises
116. **SRA** - Stringent Regulatory Authority
117. **SS** - Stability Study
118. **SVP** - Small Volume Parenterals
119. **TAT** - Turnaround Time
120. **TGA** - Therapeutic Goods Administration (Australia)
121. **TLC** - Thin Layer Chromatography
122. **TRL** - Technology Readiness Level
123. **USP** - United States Pharmacopeia
124. **USP-NF** - United States Pharmacopeia-National Formulary
125. **VICH** - Veterinary International Conference on Harmonisation
126. **WFI** - Water for Injection
127. **WIP** - Work in Progress
128. **XML** - Extensible Markup Language (used in eCTD submissions)

Case Studies

Case Study 1: Accelerated Approval of a Generic Antihypertensive Drug

Background: A pharmaceutical company sought to develop a generic version of a widely used antihypertensive drug following the expiration of its patent. The goal was to achieve bioequivalence with the reference listed drug (RLD) while meeting regulatory requirements for accelerated market entry.

Approach:

1. **API Sourcing:**

   - Partnered with a supplier holding a Type II DMF for the API to ensure compliance and speed up regulatory submissions.

2. **Formulation Development:**

   - Adopted Quality by Design (QbD) principles to optimize the formulation.
   - Conducted Design of Experiments (DoE) to identify critical process parameters (CPPs) and critical quality attributes (CQAs).

3. **Bioequivalence Study:**

   - Conducted a crossover study in healthy volunteers to demonstrate bioequivalence.
   - Results confirmed comparable pharmacokinetics (AUC and Cmax) with the RLD.

4. **Regulatory Submission:**

   - Submitted an Abbreviated New Drug Application (ANDA) to the FDA, referencing the DMF for the API.
   - Leveraged the eCTD format to streamline the submission process.

Outcome:

- The FDA approved the generic drug within nine months, enabling rapid market entry.
- The product captured significant market share due to its affordability and demonstrated efficacy.

Case Study 2: Development of a Biosimilar for Rheumatoid Arthritis

Background: A biotechnology company aimed to develop a biosimilar to a blockbuster monoclonal antibody (mAb) for rheumatoid arthritis. The reference biologic was nearing patent expiry, offering an opportunity to enter a lucrative market.

Approach:

1. **Analytical Characterization:**

   - Used advanced techniques such as LC-MS and capillary electrophoresis to ensure similarity in molecular structure, glycosylation, and aggregation profiles.

2. **Preclinical Studies:**

   - Conducted comparative in vitro studies to confirm similar binding affinity and functional activity.
   - Limited animal studies were conducted to evaluate immunogenicity.

3. **Clinical Development:**

   - Designed a Phase I/III study to demonstrate pharmacokinetic similarity and efficacy in patients.
   - The trial met all endpoints, confirming the biosimilar's equivalence in safety and efficacy.

4. **Regulatory Strategy:**

   - Followed EMA guidelines for biosimilars, including submitting a comprehensive dossier with analytical, preclinical, and clinical data.
   - Conducted additional post-marketing surveillance to monitor long-term safety.

Outcome:

- The EMA approved the biosimilar, making it one of the first affordable alternatives in its class.
- Within two years, it achieved significant adoption, reducing treatment costs by 30% across Europe.

Case Study 3: Reformulation of a Generic Antidepressant for Improved Patient Compliance

Background: A generic manufacturer sought to reformulate an antidepressant into an extended-release tablet to enhance patient compliance and differentiate it from competitors.

Approach:

1. **Formulation Innovation:**

   - Used 3D printing to create a multilayer tablet with immediate-release and extended-release components.
   - Conducted dissolution testing to optimize the drug release profile.

2. **Stability Studies:**

   - Performed accelerated and long-term stability studies to confirm the product's shelf life and resistance to environmental conditions.

3. **Market Differentiation:**

   - Highlighted the improved dosing convenience in promotional materials to healthcare providers.

4. **Regulatory Approval:**

   - Submitted the new formulation under an ANDA amendment, referencing the original bioequivalence data.

Outcome:

- The extended-release version gained market traction due to improved adherence and convenience, capturing 15% of the antidepressant market within the first year.

Case Study 4: Post-Marketing Surveillance of a Generic Anticoagulant

Background: A generic manufacturer launched a bioequivalent version of a direct oral anticoagulant. Post-marketing reports highlighted unexpected bleeding risks in certain populations.

Approach:

1. **Signal Detection:**

   - Analyzed spontaneous adverse event reports and hospital data to identify patterns.

2. **Corrective Measures:**

   - Issued a safety communication to healthcare providers, advising caution in elderly patients with renal impairment.
   - Updated the product label to include new safety warnings.

3. **Regulatory Collaboration:**

   - Submitted a detailed pharmacovigilance report to the FDA, including mitigation measures.

4. **Long-Term Monitoring:**

   - Conducted observational studies to gather more real-world safety data.

   Outcome:

- Proactive risk management restored confidence in the product, preventing market withdrawal.
- The manufacturer's transparency and responsiveness strengthened its reputation with regulators and prescribers.

Case Study 5: Complex Generic Development of a Drug-Device Combination

Background: A generic company aimed to develop a transdermal patch for hormone replacement therapy, competing with an established brand-name product.

Approach:

1. **Formulation Challenges:**

   - Overcame difficulties in achieving uniform drug dispersion in the patch matrix.
   - Used nanotechnology to enhance drug permeability through the skin.

2. **Bioequivalence Testing:**

   - Conducted in vitro permeation studies using human skin samples.
   - Performed clinical studies to confirm therapeutic equivalence.

3. **Regulatory Strategy:**

   - Submitted comprehensive documentation under an ANDA, including device performance data and quality control measures.

4. **Post-Approval Monitoring:**

   - Implemented robust pharmacovigilance systems to track adverse events related to the patch's use.

   Outcome:

- The patch gained approval and achieved rapid market penetration, offering patients a cost-effective alternative to the branded product.

www.ingramcontent.com/pod-product-compliance
Lightning Source LLC
Chambersburg PA
CBHW041305120726
48005CB00014B/1879